IN THE
OUTER COURT

BY

ANNIE BESANT

FIFTH REPRINT

The Theosophical Publishing Society
London
1915

CONTENTS.

The above are the verbatim reports of five Lectures given in the Blavatsky Lodge, London, at the Headquarters of the European Section of the Theosophical Society, during August, 1895.

LECTURE I.

PURIFICATION.

IF it were possible to place ourselves in thought at a centre in space from which we might see the course of evolution, from which we might study the history of our chain of worlds rather as they might be seen in imagination, in picture, than in the appearance that they present as physical, astral and mental, I think that thus looking outwards on these evolving groups, this evolving humanity, we might figure the whole in a picture. I see a great mountain standing in space, with a road that winds round the mountain, round and round until the summit is reached. And the turns on this road round the mountain are seven in number, and on each turn I see seven stations where pilgrims stay for a while, and within these stations they have to climb round and round.* As we trace the road

* The pilgrimage of humanity during its present cycle of evolution consists in passing seven times round a chain of seven globes ; on each globe a stay is made of many millions of years, and of these stays there are forty-nine—seven globes each dwelt on seven times.

9

upwards along this spiral track we see how it ends at the summit of the mountain—that it leads to a mighty Temple, a Temple as of white marble, radiant, which stands there shining out against the ethereal blue. That Temple is the goal of the pilgrimage, and they who are in it have finished their course—finished it so far as that mountain is concerned—and remain there only for the help of those who still are climbing. If we look more closely at the Temple, if we try to see how that Temple is built, we shall see in the midst of it a Holy of Holies, and round about the centre are Courts, four in number, ringing the Holy of Holies as concentric circles, and these are all within the Temple; a wall divides each Court from its neighbours, and to pass from Court to Court the wayfarer must go through a gateway, and there is but one in each encircling wall. So all who would reach the centre must pass through these four gateways, one by one. And outside the Temple there is yet another enclosure—the Outer Court—and that Court has in it many more than are seen within the Temple itself. Looking at the Temple and the Courts and the mountain road that winds below, we see this picture of human evolution, and the track along which the race is treading, and the Temple that is its goal. And along that road

round the mountain stands a vast mass of human
beings, climbing indeed, but climbing so slowly,
rising step after step ; sometimes it seems as though
for every step forward there is a step backward,
and though the trend of the whole mass is upwards
it mounts so slowly that the pace is scarcely
perceptible. And this æonian evolution of the race,
climbing ever upwards, seems so slow and weary
and painful that one wonders how the pilgrims
have the heart to climb so long. And tracing it
round and round the mountain millions of years
pass in the tracing, and millions of years in following
a pilgrim, and while he treads it for these millions
of years an endless succession of lives seems to
pass, all spent in climbing upwards—we weary even
in watching these vast multitudes who climb so
slowly, who tread round after round as they mount
this spiral pathway. Watching them we ask ourselves : Why is it that they climb so slowly ? How
is it that these millions of men take so long a
journey ? Why are they ever striving upwards to
this Temple that stands at the top ?

Looking at them, it seems that they travel so
slowly because they see not their goal, and
understand not the direction in which they are
travelling. And as we watch one or another on
the pathway, we see that they are always straying

aside, attracted hither and thither, and with no purpose in their going; they walk not straight onwards as though intent on business, but wander hither and thither, like children running after a blossom here, and chasing a butterfly there. So that all the time seems to be wasted, and but little progress is made when the night falls upon them and the day's march is over. Looking at them, it does not seem as though even progress in intellect, slow as that also is, made the pace very much more rapid. When we look at those whose intellect is scarcely developed, they seem after each day of life to sink to sleep almost on the place they occupied the day before; and when we glance over those who are more highly evolved so far as intellect is concerned, they too are travelling very, very slowly, and seem to make small progress in each day of life. And looking thus at them, our hearts grow weary with the climbing, and we wonder that they do not raise their eyes and understand the direction in which their path is taking them.

Now that Outer Court that some of the climbers in front are reaching, that Outer Court of the Temple, seems not only to be gained by the path that winds round and round the hill so often; for as we look at it, we see that from many points in this spiral pathway the Outer Court may be reached, and that there are briefer ways that wind not round the hill but go straight up its side, paths that may be climbed if a traveller's heart be brave and if his limbs be strong. And trying to see how men find their way more swiftly than their fellows to the Outer Court, we seem to gather that the first step is taken off this long spiral road, the first step is taken straight in the direction of this Outer Court that men can reach from so many points in the long roadway, when some Soul who has been travelling round and round, for millenniums perhaps, recognises for the first time a purpose in the journey, and catches for a moment a gleam from the Temple on the summit. For that White Temple sends rays of light over the mountain side, and now and then a traveller raises his eyes from the flowers and the pebbles and the butterflies upon the path, and the gleam seems to catch his glance and he looks upward at the Temple, and for a moment he sees it; and after that first momentary glimpse he is never again quite as he was before. For, though but for a moment, he has recognised a goal and an ending; for a moment he has seen the summit towards which he is climbing, and the pathway, steep, but so much shorter, that leads directly up the hill-side beyond which the Temple gleams. And in that moment of recognising the goal that lies in front, in that moment of understanding, if it be but for an instant, that instead of climbing round and round full seven times and making so many little circles on the upward path—for the path winds upon itself as well as round the hill, and each spiral round the mountain side has seven turns within itself and they too take long in the treading—when the Soul has caught these glimpses of its goal and of the directer pathway that leads towards it, then it understands for that moment that the pathway has a name and that the name is " Service," and that those who enter on that shorter pathway must enter it through a gate on which " Service of Man " is shining in golden letters; it understands that before it can reach even the Outer Court of the Temple it must pass through that gateway and realise that life is meant for service and not for self-seeking, and that the only way to climb upwards more swiftly is to climb for the sake of those who are lagging, in order that from the Temple more effective help may be sent down to the climbers than otherwise would be possible. As I said, it is only the flash of a moment, only a glimpse that comes and that vanishes again ; for the eye has only been caught by one of these rays of light that come down from the mountain. And there are so

many attractive objects scattered along this winding
path that the Soul's glance is easily again drawn
towards them ; but inasmuch as once it has seen
the light, there is the possibility of seeing it again
more easily, and when once the goal of achievement
and the duty and power of service has had even
this passing imaginative realisation in the Soul, then
there remains a desire to tread that shorter pathway,
and to find a way straight up the hill to the Outer
Court of the Temple.

After that first vision, gleams come from time to
time, and on day after day of this long climbing the
gleam returns to the Soul, and each glimpse perhaps
is brighter than the last, and we see that these
Souls who have just for a moment recognised that
there is a goal and purpose in life, begin to climb
with more steadfastness than their fellows ; although
they are still winding their way round the hill, we
see that they begin to practise more steadily what
we recognise as virtues, and that they give themselves more persistently to what we recognise as
religion, which is trying to tell them how they may
climb, and how the Temple may finally be won.
So that these Souls who have caught a gleam of
this possible ending, and feel some drawing towards
the path that leads thereunto, become marked out
a little from their fellows by their diligence and

heedfulness, and they go to the front of this
endless multitude that is climbing along the road;
they travel more swiftly, because there is more
purpose in their travelling, because they are taking
a direction which they begin to understand, and
they begin, though very imperfectly, to walk with
a definite aim, and to try to live with a definite
purpose. And although they scarcely yet recognise
what that purpose in the end will be—it is rather
a dim intuition than a definite understanding of the
way—still they are no longer roaming aimlessly
from side to side, sometimes a little upwards and
sometimes a little downwards; they are now
climbing steadily up the winding pathway, and each
day of life sees them climb a little faster, until
they are distinctly ahead of the multitudes in
spirituality of life, in the practice of virtue, and in
the growing desire to be of service to their fellow-
men. They are in this way travelling more swiftly
towards the summit, though still on the winding
road, and they are beginning to try to train
themselves in definite ways; they are beginning
also to try to help their neighbours, that they too
may climb with them, and as they are making their
way a little more swiftly forward they are always
reaching out helping hands to those around them,
and trying to take them with them upwards more

swiftly along the path. And presently, with those they are thus loving and serving, they are met by a form that is beautiful, though at first somewhat stern in aspect, which speaks to them and tells them something of a shorter way; we know that the form which comes to meet them is Knowledge, and that Knowledge is beginning to whisper to them something of the conditions of a swifter progress; the Religion that has been helping them in the practice of virtue is, as it were, the sister of this Knowledge, and the Service of Man is sister to it also, and the three together begin to take charge of the Soul, until at last a brighter dawning comes, and a fuller recognition, and you hear this Soul beginning to make definite to itself the purpose of its climbing, and not only to dream of a future, but to make that dream more definite in its purpose, and you find it recognising service as the law of life. Now, with deliberate intention, a promise to help in the progress of the race breathes softly forth from the lips of the Soul; and that is the first vow the Soul makes, to give itself sometime to the service of the race—a vow not yet of full purpose, but still with the promise of purpose hidden within it. It has been written in a Scripture that one of the great Ones who trod the shorter road, one of the great Ones who climbed the steeper

B

path, and Who climbed it so swiftly that He left behind Him all His race and stood alone in the forefront, the firstfruits, the promise of humanity; it is said of Him, Who in later ages was known as the Buddha, that "He perfected His vow, Kalpa after Kalpa"; for the achievement that was to crown His life had to begin with the promise of service, and it is that vow of the Soul which links it to the great Ones that have gone before, that makes as it were the link that draws it to the probationary path, the path that leads it into and across the Outer Court, up to the very gateway of the Temple itself. At last, after many lives of striving, many lives of working, growing purer and nobler and wiser, life after life, the Soul makes a distinct and clear speaking forth of a will that now has grown strong; and when that will announces itself as a clear and definite purpose, no longer the whisper that aspires, but the word that commands, then that resolute will strikes at the gateway which leads to the Outer Court of the Temple, and strikes with a knocking which none may deny—for it has in it the strength of the Soul that is determined to achieve, and that has learned enough to under-stand the vastness of the task that it undertakes. For that Soul that now is standing at the outer gateway of this Court, knows what it is striving to accomplish, realises the vastness of the difficulty that lies in front. For it means nothing less than this, that it is going to come out of its race—that race which is to be climbing round and round and round for endless millenniums, still passing from globe to globe, round that which we know as the chain, passing round and round that chain in weariful succession ; this brave Soul that now is knocking at the outer gateway means to climb that same mountain in but a few human lives, means to take step by step, breasting the hill at its steepest, the path that will lead it right upwards into the very Holy of Holies ; and it means to do within a space of time that is to be counted by but a few lives, that which the race will take myriads of lives to accomplish—a task so mighty that the brain might almost reel at its difficulty ; a task so great that of the Soul that undertakes it one would almost say that it had begun to realise its own divinity, and the omnipotence which lies enshrined within itself. For to do in a few lives from this point of the cycle that the race has reached, what the race as a whole is going to do, not only in the races that lie in front, but in the rounds that also lie in the future—to do that is surely a task worthy of a God, and the accomplishment means that the divine power is perfecting itself within the human form.

So the Soul knocks at the gateway, and the door swings open to let it through, and it passes into the Outer Court. Through that Court it has to go, traversing it step by step until it reaches the first of the gateways that lead into the Temple itself— the first of those four gateways, every one of which is one of the great Initiations, beyond the first of which no Soul may tread that has not embraced the Eternal for evermore, and that has not given up its interest in the mere transitory things that lie around. For when once a Soul has passed through the gateway of the Temple, it goeth out no more ; once it passes through that gateway into one of the inner Courts that lie beyond it and that lead to the Holy of Holies, it goes out never again. It has chosen its lot for all the millenniums to come ; it is in the place which none leaves when once he has entered it. Within the Temple itself the first great Initiation lies. But the Soul whose progress we are tracing is as yet only going to prepare itself in this Outer Court of the Temple, in order that in lives to come it may be able to ascend the seven steps to the first gateway, and await permission to pass over the threshold into the Temple itself. What then shall be its work in the Outer Court ? How shall it lead its lives therein, in order that it may become worthy to

knock at the Temple gate? That is the subject
that lies in front of us—the subject I am going to
try to put before you, if I may speak but to one
or two to whom the speaking may appeal. For
well I know, brothers and sisters mine, in depicting
this Outer Court, that I may say much that may
seem unattractive, much that may seem even
repellent. Hard enough is it to find the way to the
Outer Court; difficult enough is it to practise
religion and all the virtues which make the human
Soul fit even to knock at the gateway of this outer
stage, this Outer Court around the Temple, and
they who enter into that Court have made great
progress in their past; it may be, it will be, that
to some the life that is led therein may scarce seem
attractive—to some who have not yet definitely
recognised the aim and the end of life. For, mind
you, none are in the Outer Court save those who
have definitely vowed themselves to service, those
who have given everything, and who have asked
for nothing in return save the privilege of serving,
who have definitely recognised the transitory
nature of earthly things, who have definitely
embraced the task which they desire to achieve,
who have turned their backs on the flowery paths
which go round the mountain, and are resolutely
determined to climb straight upwards, no matter

what the cost, no matter what the strain as day after day of life swiftly succeed each other. There is to be struggle, and much of struggle, in this Outer Court, for much has to be done therein in brief space of time.

The divisions of this work that I have made are arbitrary. They are not steps, as it were, across the Court, for each of these divisions has to be taken at one and the same time and is always being worked at; it is a simultaneous training, and is not divided into stages as I have had to divide it for clearness of explanation. I have called these divisions "Purification," and "Thought Control," and the "Building of Character," and "Spiritual Alchemy," and "On the Threshold." These divisions do not mean that each is to be taken separately, because all these things have to be done at one and the same time, and the Soul that is spending its lives in the Outer Court is busy with all this work in all the lives that it spends there; it is these tasks that it must partially, at least, have learned to accomplish, ere it dare stand at the Temple gate itself. And if I take them now one by one, it is in order that we may understand them the better; but we must also understand throughout my sketching of these steps, that it is not perfect accomplishment of any one of them that the Soul must have achieved ere it may reach the gateway of the first Initiation ; but only that it must have partially accomplished, only that it must be striving with something of success, only that it must understand its work and be doing it with diligence ; when the work is perfectly accomplished, it will be in the Holy of Holies itself. Purification then is to be part of its work, self-purification, the purification of the lower nature, until every part of it vibrates perfectly in harmony with the higher, until everything is pure that belongs to the temporary part of man, to that which we call the personality, that which has not in it the permanent individual, but is only the assemblage of qualities and characteristics which that individual gathers round it in the course of each of its many lives—all the outer qualities and attributes round the Soul, all these garments in which it clothes itself, and which it carries with it often life after life, all that which it takes up as it comes back to incarnation, all that which it builds during incarnation, all that which the permanent individuality gathers round itself during earth-life and out of which it extracts the essence in order to transfuse it into its own growing and eternal Self. A phrase that very well symbolises the position of the Soul at this moment, when it has deliberately entered this Outer Court and sees the work stretching in front of it, a phrase that very well describes its attitude has been used lately by Mr. Sinnett. It is the phrase of "allegiance to the Higher Self," a useful expression, if it be understood. It means the deliberate decision that all that is temporary and that belongs to the lower personality shall be cast aside; that each life that has to be lived in this lower world shall be devoted to the single purpose of gathering together material which is useful, which then shall be handed on to the Higher One who lives and grows out of that which the lower gathers; that the lower self—realising that it is essentially one with the greater that is above it, that its only work in the world is to come here as the temporary active agency which gathers together that of which its permanent Self has need—determines that the whole of its life down here shall be spent in that service, and that the life's purpose is merely the gathering of material which then shall be taken back to the Higher, who is really the essence of itself, and who shall thus be enabled to build up the ever-growing individuality which is higher than the personality of a life. The "allegiance to the Higher Self" means the recognition of this service by the lower, the living of the lower no longer for itself but for the purpose of serving that which endures; so that all the life in the Outer Court is to be this life of definite allegiance to the Higher, and all the work that is done in the Outer Court is to be work that is done for the sake of that greater One, who is now realised as the true Self that is to endure throughout the ages, and that is to be built ever into fuller and fuller life by this deliberate, loyal service of the messenger that it sends into the outer world.

In this work that which is sometimes spoken of in the great Scriptures of the world as the preliminary step for the successful searching after the Soul, is one that I am imagining as now lying behind the Soul. You may remember to have read in one of the greatest of the Upanishads, that if a man would find the Soul the first thing to do is to " cease from evil ways "; but that I am presuming the Soul has done ere yet it has entered into the Outer Court. For those who enter it are no longer subject to the commonest temptations of earth-life; they have grown beyond those, and when they come into the incarnation which is to see them within the Outer Court, they will at least have turned from evil ways and will have ceased from walking therein with pleasure. If ever they are found in such ways at all it will be by a sudden slip immediately retrieved, and they will have been born into the world with a conscience which refuses to let them go wrong

when the right is seen before it.   And though the
conscience might have sometimes blundered in its
choice—though the conscience (not yet perfect in
its experience) might sometimes have chosen
wrongly ere entering within this Outer Court, and
even after having entered, still it would be keenly
desirous to choose rightly.. The lower self would
not deliberately go against this voice, for any one
who deliberately goes against the voice of conscience has not entered into this Outer Court at all,
nor is ready to enter it; the Souls that have
entered therein have at least chosen to strive after
the right, and they would fain obey this voice that
bids them choose it, and not deliberately disobey;
they would come into this world with that much of
their climbing behind them, and with a deliberate
will to do the highest that they see.   They now
will have to deal with subtler temptations, those in
the Outer Court; not with the grosser temptations
of the outside world, but with the subtler and keener
temptations that come to the Soul when it has to
live so swiftly through its lives, when it has to climb
so rapidly up the mountain side.   For indeed it
has no time to waste in paltering with temptations,
in slowly building virtue; it must climb onwards and
upwards ever, now it has once come within the
limits of even the Outer Court of the Temple.   And

it will find intellectual difficulties all round it and
intellectual temptations—temptations to intellectual
ambition, temptations to intellectual pride, temptations to be proud of that which it has gathered, and
to hold firmly for its own sake to that which it has
achieved. And not only will it feel this strong grip
of ambition, this grasping of the nature of pride,
that would keep for itself and would build up a
wall between itself and those who are below it,
but it will also have a desire for knowledge, a desire
for knowledge for itself, a desire for knowledge
that it may gain and hold rather as against the
world than for it. And this temptation veils itself
as love of knowledge for its own sake, and love of
truth for its own sake, and oftentimes the Soul
finds, as its eyesight grows keener and clearer, that
this supposed aspiring love is often only the desire
to be separated from its fellows, to have what they
do not share and to enjoy what it does not give
to them. This separateness is one of the great
dangers of the growing Soul, the pride in separateness and the desire to be separated—the desire to
grow and to learn and to achieve in order that it
may possess ; this is one of the temptations that
will touch it even when it has passed through the
gateway of the Outer Court. For the Soul will see
knowledge within its grasp, and will desire to hold

it ; will see power within its grasp and will desire to have it ; desire, not only for the sake of service, but also partly because these make itself the greater, and it is inclined to build this wall about itself so that it may keep for self that which it has achieved ; presently it begins to understand that if it would ever traverse the Outer Court and reach the gateway that is shining ahead of it, it must get rid of all this intellectual ambition, and all this intellectual pride, and all this desire for knowledge which it will hold for itself, and everything that makes it separate from its brother Souls ; then it will begin to purify its intellectual nature, it will begin to scrutinise the motives which impel it to effort and the motives which move it to action, and it will begin carefully to look at itself in the light that shines from the Temple, and that is ever coming through the Temple windows and illuminating this Outer Court with rays of spiritual Life ; light in which every shadow seems to be darker, and the very things that look bright in the lower world are seen after all to be shadows and not to be rays of light at all. Then the Soul will realise that this desire-nature which it has brought with it, and which mixes itself with the intellectual, that this desire-nature has to be purified from every touch of the personal self ; it will deliberately begin this work of purification, it will deliberately and consciously and steadfastly set itself to work to purge out of itself everything which strives to take for the personality, and everything which makes it in any sense separate from those that are below it as well as from Those that are above. For this the Soul learns—and it is one of the lessons of the Outer Court—that there is only one way which these doors swing open, the doors that shut it out of the Temple, and that is by the breaking down of the walls that separate it from its fellows that are below. Then the walls that separate it from those that are in front disappear, absorbed as it were by their own action; for that gate that has to be passed through is a gate that will only open to him who desires passage, as he breaks down the walls of his own nature and is willing to share with all that which he achieves.

Thus he begins this work of purifying the desire-nature, and he takes this lower self in hand to purge out of it everything which is personal. How shall he purify himself? He does not want to destroy; for that which he has gathered together is experience, and experience has been built into faculty and transmuted into power, and he now needs all these powers that he has been gathering during the climb that lies below him, and it will not do to destroy all that he has gathered; he wants to take these powers on with him, but to take them purified instead of foul. How then shall he purify them? It would be so much easier to destroy; it would need so much less patience to kill some of these qualities that he has; he feels as if he could strike at them and slay them, and so be rid of them. But it is not thus that he can enter into the Temple; for he must take there as his sacrifice that has to be offered on the very threshold of the Temple, everything that he has gathered in his past, that he has turned into power and faculty; he must not go in thither empty-handed, he must take with him all that he has gathered in his lower life. So that he dares not destroy; he must perform the harder work of purification; he must keep the essence of all the qualities, while he strikes away from them everything that is personal. All the lessons he has learnt of virtue and of vice, all these are the experiences that in the pilgrimage behind him he has gathered; he must take the essence of every quality with him, for these are the results of all his climbing; but he must take them as pure gold to the altar, and no dross must be mingled with the gold.

Let us take one or two of these qualities in order to see clearly what purification means; for if we understand it as to one or two qualities, then at our leisure we can work it out for the rest, and the lesson is all-important as to how the purification is to be worked.

Let me take first a mighty force which is in every human being, which he develops in the low stages of his growth, which he carries on with him as he evolves, and which it is now his work to purify. Let us take the quality that in its lowest stage we know as anger, as wrath, as that tremendous power that the man develops, by which he fights his way through the world, by which he struggles, and by which he oftentimes overcomes all opposition : that tremendous energy of the Soul rushing out through the lower nature and breaking a man's way for him through difficulties in the earlier stages of his growth ere yet he has learned to guide and to control it; an undisciplined energy, destructive because it is undisciplined ; a tremendous force, valuable because it is force, although destructive in its workings as we see it in the lower world. The man ere yet he has entered into the Outer Court has somewhat changed that energy of the Soul; he has changed it into a virtue, a very real virtue, and he has had this virtue long as his possession in the outside world ; then it went by the names (when it had reached the stage of virtue)

of noble indignation, of passion against injustice,
of hatred of all that was wrong, and that was base,
and that was vile, and that was cruel, and it did
good service in the outer world under these many
forms of destructive energy.   For this man, ere yet
he came into the Outer Court, had been working
for the world, and had been practising this virtue;
and when he saw the cruelty that was done upon the
weak his passion broke forth against it, and when
an injustice was wrought by a tyrant then he rose
up against it in indignation; he had learned, as he
practised this virtue, to purify it from much of the
dross; for the anger that he had in his earlier lives
was anger for himself—he was wrathful when he
was injured, he struck back when some one struck
at him; but he had long ago conquered that mere
brute wrath in the lower nature which guards itself
by destructive energy against a wrong, and
pays back evil with evil and hate with hate.
Before he entered the Outer Court he had
passed   beyond   that   earlier   stage,   and   had
learned   to   some   extent   to   transform   that
energy of anger in him; he had purified it to
a great extent from the personal element, and he
had learned to be angry less because he himself
was injured, than because some one else was
wronged; he had learned to be indignant less

because he suffered, than because some one else was put to pain; and when he saw some cruel creature trampling on a helpless one, he sprang forward to rescue that helpless creature and struck at the wrong-doer and cast him to one side; in that way he had used the higher anger to conquer the lower, in that way he had used the nobler passion to slay the more animal passion of his lower life, and he had learned in these lives that now lie far behind him, to get rid so far of the grosser qualities of the passion; he had learned to be no longer angry for himself, but angry only for those whom he desired to help. For he was a man, remember, who had long recognised service as duty, and one of his ways of service was by striking down oppressors and by casting aside those who were inflicting suffering; this anger of his blazed up hotly against all forms of wrong, and he worked for the weaker, and perchance did-hero's work in the world. But within that calmer atmosphere of the Court of the Temple, illuminated by the rays of absolute compassion shining forth from the Holy of Holies, there is no place for anger of any sort, even though the anger be purged from personal antagonism. For the aspirant has now to learn that those who do the wrong are also his brothers, and that they suffer more in their wrong-doing than do

c

their fellow-men by the injury that they may inflict;
he has to learn that this noble indignation of
his, and this passion of his against the wrong, and
this fire that blazed forth to consume a tyranny
that touched not himself, that that is not the
characteristic of the Soul that is striving onwards
towards the Divine; for the Divine Life loves all
the children that It sends into the world, no matter
what may be their position, nor how low the grade
of their evolution.   For the Love of the Divine that
emanated all has nothing outside Itself.   The Life
that is Divine is the core of everything that exists,
and there is God present in the heart of the evil-
doer as well as in the heart of the saint.   Within the
Outer Court the Divine must be recognised, no
matter how thick are the veils that hide it, for there
the eyes of the Spirit are to be opened, and there
is to be no veil between it and the Self of other
men; therefore this noble indignation is to be
purified until it is purged of everything that is of
anger, and is changed into an energy that leaves
nothing outside its helpful range; until this great
energy of the Soul become an energy that is
absolutely pure, that goes out to help the tyrant as
well as the slave, and that embraces within its
limit the one who is trampling as well as the one
who is trampled; for the Saviours of men choose

not whom They will serve—Their service is a service that knows no limitations, and They that are the servants of all hate none within the Universe. That which once was anger has to become by purification, protection for the weak, impersonal opposition to strong evil-doing, perfect justice to all.

And so again as he does with anger he must do with love, with love that began showing itself forth in him in its lowest and poorest form as the Soul was beginning to grow, that showed itself forth, perhaps, in forms that were foul and in forms that were vile, that only knew the goings outward to another, and that in its self-gratification troubled not much as to what happened even to that which it loved; as the Soul has been growing upwards, love has changed its character, has become nobler, less selfish, less personal, until it has attached itself to the higher elements in the beloved instead of to the outer casing, and the love that was sensual has become moralised and purified. It must be made still purer when the candidate has come within the Outer Court of the Temple; he must carry in with him love, but it is love that must have begun to lose its exclusiveness; it is love which must keep its fire ever burning more warmly, but the warmth must spread out further and furthe:

and be purified from everything of lower nature ; and that means that the love shall be a love that in going out to others shall always seek to serve them rather than to serve itself, shall always seek how much it may give to them rather than how much it may take from them, and so a love that will be becoming gradually Divine in its essence, going out according to the measure of the need rather than according to the richness of the return.

As the Soul is thus striving after purification, it will have certain tests that it will apply to all this process through which it is passing itself, and when it is at work using its energy in order to accomplish some service to man it will bring to that service the Ithuriel spear of the absence of personality, and will see what starts up in answer to the touch of the spear. If it find that when it is doing service, when its energy is going out to achieve something that it realises as good, if in testing that action and its motive it find that the " I " is subtly mingled with the energy ; if it find that it looks less for the success of the working than for the success of the operator ; if it find that when it fails in its own working but sees that work accomplished by another, there is something of disappointment mingling in the cup of its delight at seeing the work achieved ; then it knows that the personality is still lingering in it, that if it were what it ought to be, it would care only for the triumph of the service, and not for having itself contributed to the triumph. And if it find that in personal failure there is still a sting of disappointment; if it find that from the failure of its own outgoing energy there comes back to it something of depression, something of discouragement, something which clouds for a moment its peace and its serenity, then it realises that in that sting and in that cloud there is still a part of the personality that needs to be destroyed, and it sets to work to get rid also of that weakness, and to clear away that cloud from the eyes of the Soul. And if it find, when it is measuring and testing the nature of its love, that there is there also a little chill, a little feeling of disappointment, when that which it has loved remains indifferent to its giving, though it has served nobly and loved greatly; if it find that the outward flowing of its love is inclined to shrink backward and to check its course, because those to whom it gives the love answer not back with love in return; then, again, this Soul—that is so stern to itself whilst so compassionate to all other Souls—knows that in this also there is a subtle lingering of the personality, and that it is still working for something for itself, and is not finding its highest joy in the mere glory of the giving. Then,

again, it sets to work, this Soul that is in the Outer
Court of the Temple, to purify away that lingering
part of the personality, until the love flows out,
never asking whether aught comes back to it, never
waiting to see if answer is there; for it knows in
truth that the need for love is greatest where
answer of love there is none, and it knows that
those Souls have the greatest need to receive who
themselves at present give nothing to the love that
helps.

In this way the Soul deliberately labours for
growth; deliberately it works at itself, purifying
always the lower nature with unceasing effort and
with untiring demand; for ever it is comparing
itself not with those who are below it but with
Those who are above it, ever it is raising its eyes
towards Those who have achieved, and not looking
downwards towards those who are still only climbing upwards towards the Outer Court.   And it can
never for a moment rest, it can never be content,
until it sees itself ever coming nearer to its goal,
until there is less opposition within itself to the
passing through it of the light of the Holy Ones
who have become Divine.

Within this Outer Court the temptations of men
are by their virtues, not by their vices; subtle
temptations assail their nature that appear like

angels of light ; and ever the temptation comes to
these Souls that are passing onwards through that
which is greatest in them, by that which is noblest
in them ; it is their virtues which are taken, and,
using the advantage of their lack of knowledge,
these are turned into temptations ; for they have
grown beyond the point where vice could touch
or tempt them, and it is only by using the mask of
virtue that illusion may avail to lead them astray.
That is why they learn to be so hard upon themselves, that is why they are so ceaseless in the demands that they make upon themselves ; they
know full well by their own slipping, and by the
slipping of their comrades, that those virtues that
in the lower world are difficult of achievement are
the very things that become easy to those within
the Outer Court, and that these are then, as it were,
stolen by the enemy, in order that he may turn them
into temptations by which also they may be made
to falter on the Path. Therefore it is that they
learn that the only safety for them is in living within the light of the Higher Self ; therefore it is that
they realise that they dare not stand at the Gate of
the Temple until that Light shines out radiantly
within them, and therefore they are ever striving to
make themselves absolutely translucent. For how
shall they dare to pass into a Light to which every-

thing that is light here is but as shadow; how shall they dare to pass into a Light at which no impure eyes can look for the dazzling quality of its rays, making all that we call virtue seem imperfect of achievement, and all that we call beauty but as ugliness and as flatness; how shall they dare to go within the Temple, where the Eyes of the Master shall rest upon them, and they shall stand, the Soul naked, in His presence; how shall they dare to stand there, if within the heart there be still one stain of imperfection, and if when He looks into the heart there be found there one soil to offend the purity of His gaze?

Therefore is it that in this Outer Court things that are painful in the world outside become as joy, and the suffering that purifies is the most welcome of friends; therefore is it that the pattern of all Yogîs, He Who is said to be Himself the Great Yogî, the Master and the Patron of all; therefore is it that He stands ever in the burning-ground, and that flames play ever round His presence and consume everything that they touch. For in the hearts of those who are in the Outer Court there are still hidden places into which the light has not yet pierced, and the final purification ere they enter into the Temple comes from these living flames of the Lord Himself, and they burn up all that lurks

unseen in the hidden chambers of the heart of him
who is to be a disciple. He has given himself to
his Lord and he keeps nothing back; in that
mighty burning-ground, which stands before the
gateway of the Temple, is the blazing fire through
which all must pass ere yet the Temple Gate can
open for them; it is beyond the fire and in it that
the figure of the Great Yogî is seen, from Whom
those flames come forth, taking their purifying
power from the glory of His Feet. It is from Him,
the Great Guru, that comes this final purification
of the disciple, and then he enters within the gateway that shuts him out for ever from all the in-
terests of the lower world, save that of service;
which separates him from all human desires save as
he works for the redemption of Humanity; there
remains nothing on earth which is able to attract
him, because he has seen the Face of his Lord and
before that all other lights grow dim.

LECTURE II

Thought Control.

PERHAPS in the subject or rather the section of the subject that I have to deal with to-night there will be almost more of difference than in any other part of it, between the view that would be taken, say, by a thoughtful well-balanced virtuous man in the world and the view which is taken by the Occultist. I shall want, as it were, to lead you step by step from the beginning, and to show you how this change of standpoint occurs; for it is perhaps especially in regard to the mind, the position that the mind holds towards the man, the place that it has in his developing nature, the functions that it performs and the way in which it performs them —it is on these matters that so much of difference will arise according to the position of the thinker, according to the view that he takes of the world at large and of the part which he there is called upon to play. Let us for a moment, in order to realise just where we are in this matter, let us for a moment try to think how a good and just and intellectual man—that is a man who is distinctly not careless nor frivolous nor worldly in the ordinary sense of the terms—let us consider how such a person, sober in his judgment and balanced in his thinking, would regard this question of mental self-control. A good man, a man who has deliberately set before himself an ideal of virtue which he strives to realise, a view of duty which he endeavours to discharge, such a man in the course of the forming of this ideal and the marking out of this line of duty, will recognise that what we call the lower nature is a thing to be mastered, to be controlled. On that no question will arise at all. The passions and the appetites of the body, the lower emotions which hurry people away without reflection and without thought, all that side of the man's nature which is played upon from without so that he acts without consideration, as it would be said, without reflection and without thought—our virtuous man will most certainly say that this is to be dominated and to be kept under control. He will speak of that as the lower nature, and he will seek to reduce it to obedience to the higher. If we examine carefully the position of such a man, we shall find that what we mean in ordinary parlance

by a self-controlled man is a man who exercises this
mental control over the lower nature, so that the
mind controls the desires ; when we say " self-controlled " it is the man that is thought of as the self
who is controlling.   More than that ; if we look at
him a little more closely we shall see that what we
call the strong will, what we call the formed
character, a character which acts along certain
definite lines of conduct, a will which, under
very difficult circumstances, is still able to guide the
nature of which it forms a part along a clear and
definite line, we shall find that we mean by such a
person that he is one in whom the mind has been
largely developed, so that when he comes to act and
to decide upon an action he is not determined in
his action by the external circumstances, he is not
determined in his action by the various attractions
that may surround him outside, he is not determined in his action by the answer of the animal
nature to those attractions ; he is determined, we
shall find, by a mass of experiences recorded in
what is called his memory, remembrance of past
occurrences, comparison of the results which flowed
from these occurrences ; the mind has worked upon
all of these, has, as it were, arranged them and compared them the one with the other, and has drawn
from them a definite result by an intellectual and

logical effort. This result remains in the mind as
a rule of conduct, and when the man is under circumstances that are disturbing, circumstances that
would overcome what is called a weak will, circumstances that would perhaps lead astray just an
average person, this stronger and more developed
mind—having laid down a rule of conduct at which
it has arrived in a moment of calm, in moments
when the desire-nature is not actively at work, in
moments when it is not surrounded by temptations
—this mind guides its conduct by this rule of conduct which has thus been ascertained and laid
down, and does not permit itself to be turned out
of its course by the attractions or by the impulses
of the moment.   In dealing with such a person you
can often forecast what he will do ; you know the
principles upon which his conduct is based ; you
know the lines of thought which dominate his
mind ; and you feel pretty sure—looking at this
character, which is definite and formed and strong
—you feel pretty sure that no matter what may be
the outside temptations, that man will fulfil in the
moment of strife the ideal which he conceived in
the moments of calm and of reflection.   And in
speaking of a self-controlled man this is what we
generally mean ; he is a man who has reached this
stage of development, which is by no means a low

stage you will observe, in which he has deliberately set himself to work to conquer and to rein in and to manage this lower nature, so that when it is most stimulated into action from without, the Soul shall be able to hold its own against the inrushing of temptation, and the man shall act on a noble standard, no matter what may be the temptations that surround him to act basely, or in accordance with the temptings of the lower nature.

So far then we have taken what may well be called a virtuous man, this man of high character, of clear thought, of sound judgment, who is by no means driven hither and thither by circumstances, nor by impulses, as is the normal unregulated or ill-regulated nature. But there is another stage to which this man may come, He may come into contact with a great philosophy of life which explains to him something more of the workings of the mind; he may come, for instance, into contact with the great Theosophical teachings, whether as expounded in ancient or modern books, whether he gains them from India, from Egypt, from Greece, or from modern Europe. And in that philosophy he may learn a new view of the Universe, and it may largely modify his own position.

Suppose that such a man should come into the Theosophical Society and should accept its main

D

teachings, he will then begin to realise, far more than he did before he studied things from a Theosophical standpoint, the enormous influence of his thoughts. He will begin to understand that when his mind is working, it is exercising that creative power which will be so familiar probably to most of you; that the mind is actually making definite existences or entities, that in this creative action of the mind it is constantly sending out into the world around active entities that work for good or for evil, and that work often upon the minds and upon the lives of people with whom the creator of these entities does not come into personal contact. He will begin to understand that it is by no means necessary in this affecting of the minds of others that he should put his thought either into spoken or into written words. Nor is it necessary that his thought should show itself in action, so that his example may become potent for good or for evil. He realises that he may be an exceedingly obscure person as the world counts obscurity; that he may be quite out of sight of the public; that he may only influence an exceedingly small circle of his friends and relatives who come into personal contact with himself; but he will see that although he does not come into contact with people personally, although he does not reach them by written or spoken words,

he has a power which transcends either the force
of example or the forces of speech or of tongue,
and that sitting alone and isolated from men, so far
as the physical world is concerned, he may be exercising a force potent for good or for evil; he may
be purifying or fouling the minds of his generation; he may be contributing to, helping, or hinder-
ing the progress of the world; he may be raising
his race a little higher or depressing it a little
lower; and quite apart from everything that ordinary people recognise as the force of precept or of
example, he may be influencing the mind of his
time by these subtle energies of thought, by these
active forms that go into the world of men, that
work the more forcibly in that they are invisible,
and exercise the wider influence just because they
are so subtle that they are unrecognised by the
masses whom they affect.

In this way, as he grows in his knowledge,
thought will for him take on a new complexion, and
he will realise how mighty is the responsibility of
thought, that is, how great is the responsibility
which is upon his own shoulders, simply as exercising these faculties of the mind. He will realise
that his responsibility extends much farther than
he can see; that he is responsible in a very real
way often for the crimes that happen in the society

to which he belongs, as well as for the deeds of heroism that may also happen in that society. He will grasp that great principle that it by no means follows that the man who does an act is wholly and solely responsible for the act which he performs; but that every act is a coming into manifestation, a veritable incarnation, of ideas, and that every one who takes part in the generation of the ideas takes part in the responsibility for the action. Understanding that, and taking this wider view of life, he would begin to be very careful about his thoughts, he would begin to realise that he must control his thoughts, and this goes beyond the view which was taken by our man of the world; further, as he understands that he must control his thoughts and is responsible for his thoughts, as he begins to realise that not only is he responsible for these thoughts, and therefore must have some choice as to the kind of thoughts that he generates, he also finds if he studies a little further that the kind of thoughts that he attracts to himself from the outer world will be very largely determined by the nature of the thoughts that he himself generates. So that he is not only a magnet sending out lines of thought-force over the area of his magnetic field, but he is also a magnet attracting towards himself the substances which answer to the magnetic force

that he sends out; whether then his mind be full
of good thoughts or of base thoughts will very
largely depend upon the lines along which his own
mental force is exercised, and he will begin to
understand that in generating a good thought he is
not only discharging his supreme duty to his fellows,
but that—as ever happens when man is in
harmony with the Divine Law—he himself is gaining by that which he gives; in each case in which
he gives to the world a noble thought, he has set
up in himself an attractive centre to which other
noble thoughts will come of their own accord,
drawn, as it were, by magnetic affinity, so that his
own mind will be helped and strengthened by these
thoughts that flow into it from without. He
recognises also with pain and shame that when he
sends out into the world a foul thought he has
made in his own consciousness a similar centre,
which will attract the baser thoughts in the atmosphere, and so increase his own tendencies towards
evil as the others increase his tendencies towards
good. And as he learns to understand this mental
brotherhood which binds all men together, you will
realise that he will change his mental attitude, that
he will feel this responsibility of giving out and
of taking in, that he will recognise these ties that
stretch out in every direction from him and also

stretch out from every direction towards him, that he in his daily life will begin to deal more with thought than he will with action, and to understand that in that region of the invisible there are generated all the forces which come down into the psychic and the physical life.

But there is a step further when he comes within the Outer Court. He is now a candidate—as you will remember from what we said last week—he is now a candidate to enter on that steeper and shorter Path leading upwards, nay, he is on the probationary stage of that Path itself. Something more then will come to him than this recognition, that we have seen belongs to the man who is beginning to understand something of the nature of the life around him. And this candidate, who has stepped across the threshold of the Outer Court, finds that he recognises something that is behind the mind, something which is greater than the mind, something to which the mind bears a relation which has an analogy to the relation which is borne to the mind itself by the lower desire-nature; that just as in the course of growth a man recognises the mind above the desires, so when he has stepped across the threshold, and even before he takes that step— for it is the recognition of this fact which leads to the gateway and partly opens that gateway to him

—he realises that this mind which seemed so great, this mind which seemed so mighty, which seemed to him in the days that lie but a little way behind to be the ruler of the world and its monarch, that mind of which it was said by a thinker that " there is nothing great in the Universe but man, and there is nothing great in man but mind," that all this comes from a view that is taken from below with a sight that is blinded, and that when the sight begins to clear itself it is seen that there is something greater in this Universe than this mind which seemed to be the greatest thing in man—something which is sublimer, something which is vaster, something which only shines out for a moment, and then again is veiled. He recognises dimly, poorly, not yet by knowledge but by hearsay, that he has caught a glimpse of the Soul, that to him a ray of light has come downwards into the mind from something that is above it, and yet that he dimly seems to feel in some strange sense is itself, is identical with it. So that at first there will be a confusion and a groping in the darkness, between this which seems to be himself although he had thought he himself was mind, and yet which seems so much greater than the mind. So that it seems to be himself, and yet greater than he, and he knows not at first whence this gleam may come, and whether the hope that it raised in him is a dream and nothing more.

But before we can deal with the facts clearly at all, we must try to see what we mean by these words "Mind" and "Soul," what we mean when we speak of "Consciousness"; for these words, if we are to understand, must not for us be counters to play with, but real coins that represent something that we have of mental wealth, of ideas. So let us take these words for a moment and see what is meant by them, or at least what I will mean by them in using them, so that what I say will be clear, whether you agree with the definitions or not. I define the Soul as that which individualises the Universal Spirit, which focuses the Universal Light into a single point; which is, as it were, a receptacle into which is poured the Spirit; so that that which in Itself is universal, poured into this receptacle appears as separate, identical in its essence always but separated now in its manifestation; the purpose of this separation being that an individual may develop and grow; that there may be an individualised life potent on every plane in the Universe; that it may know on the physical and on the psychical planes as it knows on the spiritual, and have no break in consciousness of any kind; that it may make for itself the vehicles that it needs for acquiring consciousness beyond its own plane, and then may gradually purify them one by one until they no longer act as blinds or as hindrances, but as pure and translucent media through which all knowledge on every plane may come. But in using the word or image "receptacle" I may mislead you; and here is the difficulty with all expressions fitted for intellectual thinking; that if one takes an image which on one point is applicable we find it on another misleading. For this process of individualisation is by no means the making of a receptacle and the pouring of something into it, so that at once that which is poured into it takes definite outline and shape, moulded into the shape of the vessel. What happens is more analogous to the way in which some great system, some Solar System say, is formed; if you throw your imagination backwards in time, you might imagine space in which nothing is visible; and you might then imagine that in that space—where there seemed to be emptiness, but where there is really all fulness, only fulness invisible to the eye—that in that space there comes a slight mist, too delicate almost to be called a mist at all, and yet that is the nearest word that would explain this beginning of aggregation; and then as you watch it, the mist grows denser and denser, and denser and denser as the time goes on, aggregating more and more closely together and becoming more separated from the space around it; till that which seemed but the faintest of shadows begins to take to itself a shape, becoming more and more definite as it proceeds, until if you were watching this building of the worlds, you would see the nebula become denser and denser, and separating itself off more definitely in space, until a system was formed with a central sun and planets all around it. And so it seems, however blunderingly put, is this coming of Spirit into individualisation; it is like the faint appearance of a shadow in the universal void which is the fullest of all fulnesses, and then this shadow becomes a mist, and then it takes to itself clearer and clearer form, becoming more and more definite as evolution proceeds, until there is an individual, a Soul, where at first there was only the faintest shadow of a growing mist: such is the process (in picture) of this forming of the individual consciousness. And if you can take that thought of it for the moment, you will perchance realise how it is that the Soul is formed in the long course of evolution, and that this Soul is not a thing complete at first, plunging down like a diver into the ocean of matter, but is slowly, slowly builded, or densified, if I may still use the image, until out of the Universal it becomes

the individual, and an individual that is ever growing as its evolution proceeds. That Soul lasts, as
we know, from life to life through endless years,
through countless centuries. It is the growing
individual, and its consciousness is the consciousness of all that lies behind it in the process of its
growth. The Soul is that entity, growing mighty
to-day in some of the Sons of Men; it has behind
it a storied past ever present to this consciousness
which has grown so wide during its treading of the
long path over which it has travelled; it has this
vast consciousness, taking all its lives into itself and
realising all its past. And then as each new birth
comes, and new experience has to be gathered, this
Soul which has been growing through the ages
casts out into new vestures a part of itself, to gather
for it new experience; and this part of itself which
is flowing outwards on to the lower planes that
there it may increase the knowledge out of which
the Soul is to grow still greater, this part of itself
flowing outwards is what we call the Mind in man;
it is the part of the Soul that is working in the brain,
confined in the brain, sorely fettered by the brain,
with what is literally the burden of the flesh upon it,
making its consciousness dimmer, for it cannot
pierce through this thicker veil of matter; all that
greatness that we know as the Mind is only this

struggling part of the Soul, working in this brain for purposes of the Soul's growth. And as it works in it, it shows out the powers of the Soul, for it is the Soul itself, although clothed in this limitation of matter, and as much of the Soul as can manifest through that brain is the mind of the person that we know, and sometimes much will manifest and sometimes little, according to the state of evolution which has been reached. But what the man in the Outer Court understands is that it is this Soul which is himself, and that the mind is only its passing manifestation. And then he begins to understand that just as the body and the desire-nature are to be subject to the mind, which is part of the Soul in prison, so that mind itself is to be subject to the great Soul of which it is only the projected representative of the moment ; that it is only an instrument, only an organ of the Soul, manifested for the sake of the work it performs, and for that which it has to gather and to draw back into the Soul, which is itself.

Realising that, then, what will be the position of our candidate ? The mind learns; as this mind comes into contact with the outer world, it gathers together facts, it arranges them, it tabulates them, it forms its judgments on them, and carries on all the rest of its intellectual processes; the result of

this activity passes upwards, passes along this
expansion of the Soul upwards into the Soul itself
—or rather inwards; it is this which the Soul takes
with it into Devachan, and there works upon it all
to change it into wisdom. For wisdom is very
different from learning. Learning is all that mass
of facts, and of judgments on the facts, and of
conclusions drawn therefrom; wisdom is the
extracted essence of the whole, that which the Soul
has gathered out of all these experiences, and it is,
as you are aware, its work in Devachan to turn
these experiences into wisdom. But our candidate,
who knows all this, will realise that it is this Soul
which is "I"; the Soul which has come through
all these past lives and has been building itself in
the coming, that is the "I" that is himself, so far
as he yet can see. And then he begins to understand why it is said that at the very outset he has
to distinguish between the "I" that endures and
this mind which is only a passing manifestation
of the "I". Mind is the Soul's manifestation in
the world of matter, it is manifested there in order
that it may work for the purposes of the Soul;
and then he may begin to realise why it is that when
the pupil sends out to the Master his first cry for
teaching, when having found his way into the Outer
Court, he cries: "O Teacher, what shall I do to

reach to wisdom ?   O Wise One, what, to gain
perfection ? "—those words that sound strange at
first come from the lips of the Wise One : " Search
for the Paths. But, O Lanoo, be of clean heart
before thou startest on thy journey. Before thou
takest thy first step, learn to discern the real from
the false, the ever-fleeting from the everlasting." *
And then the Teacher goes on to explain the
difference between learning and wisdom—what is
ignorance, what is knowledge, and what is the
wisdom that succeeds them both. And the dis-
tinction is drawn between the mind—the mind that
is " like a mirror ; it gathers dust while it reflects " ;
the mind that needs the " breezes of Soul-wisdom
to brush away the dust of our illusions." And on
those words the candidate, if he be wise, reflects.
What is this difference between the real and the
fleeting, and why is it connected with the manifestation of the mind ?   What is this difference
between the mirror that reflects and the Soul that
needs to dust the mirror if illusion is to be gotten
rid of ? For what part can it be which this mind
plays, which seems so mighty a function in man
that it stood as the man himself in the lower
world ? What is its function after all if the first
step upon the Path is to distinguish what is illusory

* *Voice of the Silence* (Lotus Leaf Edition), pp. 34, 35.

from what is real, and the mind in some subtle fashion is connected with the making of the illusion ? And there are other words which he remembers he has heard as coming also from the lips of these Masters of Wisdom. He remembers a strange word that came which spoke of the Râjah of the senses, ruler and king of the lower nature, but no friend of the disciple ; he remembers that— in those very words where this Râjah of the senses is spoken of, at the outset of the teaching—he remembers that he was bidden to seek out that Râjah of the senses so as to understand him, for he is "the Thought-Producer, he who awakes illusion"; and the disciple is told that the "mind is the great slayer of the Real. Let the disciple slay the slayer." * Here then we seem to be on the track of some thought that will be illuminative to the candidate who is to seek out the Râjah of the senses; that Râjah, or king, of the senses is the thought-producer, and he who produces thought is he who awakes illusion, it is he who slays the Real. For in the Spirit-World there is Reality; as the process of differentiation proceeds, illusion is produced, and it is this mind, this growing mind, that makes the illusion. It is this growing mind that has endless images and pictures, that has the image-

* *Voice of the Silence*, p. 13.

making faculty which we speak of as imagination, that has the reasoning faculty which builds on the airy picture that it has made—it is this which is the real creator of illusion, it is this which slays the Real, so far as the disciple is concerned, and his first work as disciple will be to slay the slayer. For unless he can get rid of this illusive power of the mind, he will never be able to penetrate beyond the Outer Court. And then listening still to the Teacher, he hears a voice which bids him seek to blend his Mind and Soul.* His work then will be to make some change in this lower mind which shall make it capable of blending with the higher, some destruction of its illusory power which shall enable it to know its own parent from whom it comes, that the Father and the Son may once more become one.

And then he hears a teaching which in mystic language says to him that he must destroy the lunar body, that he must cleanse the mind-body;† and studying that, and striving to understand what it means, he learns from many an allegory and from many a symbol, now becoming familiar to him in his lessons, he learns that what is called the lunar body is that body which belongs to Kâma or Desire, that which is spoken of as the astral man;

* *Ibid.*, p. 36.   † *Ibid*, p. 22.

and he learns that that is to be destroyed, and that the mind-body is to be cleansed. " Cleanse thy mind-body," the Teacher tells him, for only by cleansing away the dust of illusion will it be possible for that mind-body to re-enter itself, will it be possible for it to be blended with its Soul. And now he begins to understand the work that lies before him in the Outer Court with regard to this mind. He begins to realise that he himself, this living Soul that has been climbing through the centuries, has been putting out this force of itself in order to create an instrument for its own use, a servant which is to be controlled; that instead of the mind being master, the mind is to be an obedient slave, instrument in the hand that holds it, servant to him who sent it forth; and as that grows upon him, the nature of his task unfolds itself before him and he begins to train his mind. And in seeking to do this at first he will have to begin with very simple matters; he will find that this mind is always running about from one thing to another, hard to control and difficult to curb, as Arjuna found it five thousand years ago, restless and uneasy, turbulent and difficult to restrain ; and he will begin at first by training it, as you would train a steed that you are breaking in for your riding, to go definitely along the road that you

E

choose, not leaping over hedge and ditch, and racing across country in every direction, but going along the road that is chosen by the rider, along that and along no other.   And so this candidate of ours in his daily life—for he has to work out all this in the life of the world—will gradually, as he works, train his mind in thinking consecutively and thinking definitely, and he will not permit himself to be led astray by all the manifold temptations around him, to the scattering of thought in every direction. He will refuse to scatter thought ; he will insist that it shall pursue a definite path ; he will decline to take all his knowledge in scraps, as though he had no power of following a sustained argument ; he will put aside the endless temptations that surround him in this superficial age and time ; he will read by choice and by deliberate motive—for it is here that the thought of the candidate is trained—he will read with deliberate motive sustained arguments, long lines of argument which train the mind in going along one definite line for a considerable period, and he will not permit it to leap from one thing to another rapidly, thus intensifying the restlessness which is an obstacle in his path, and which will block his way utterly until it is overcome.

And thus daily, and month by month, and year by year, he will work at his mind, training it in these consecutive habits of thought, and he will learn to choose that of which he thinks ; he will no longer allow thoughts to come and go ; he will no longer permit a thought to grip him and hold him ; he will no longer let a thought come into the mind and fix itself there and decline to be evicted ; he will be master within his own house. He may have troubles in his daily life ; it matters not ; they will help him in this training of the mind. And when these troubles are very pressing, when these anxieties are very trying, when he finds himself inclined to look forwards and to worry over the troubles that are coming to him a few days, or a few weeks, or a few months hence, he will say : " No ; no such anxiety shall remain within my mind ; no such thought shall have shelter within my mind ; within this mind nothing stays that is not there by my choice and my invitation, and that which comes uninvited shall be turned outside the limits of my mind." People lie awake at night, filled with anxious thoughts, people are half killing themselves not by their troubles, but by the worries that those troubles cause within the mind ; all that kind of thing will be put an end to by the candidate, for he will refuse to permit any action which is not by his own consent, and he will shut and lock the doors of the mind against all these thoughts that

press in thither uninvited; this will be a definite
training, a difficult and a long training, for the
thoughts break in and he has to turn them out.
And over and over and over again he must do it,
and there is no way in which it can be done save by
taking such a thought, whenever it comes in, and
as often as it comes in, and deliberately declining
to give it harbourage.   You will say, "How?"
Probably at first most easily by giving the mind
something else to think about; later on by simply
refusing to admit it.   But until the candidate has
grown strong enough thus to shut and lock the
doors of his mind and remain therein undisturbed,
he may do wisely to substitute one thought for
another, and always to substitute some high thought
which deals with the permanent for the thought he
wants to get rid of, which deals with the transitory.
For then it will serve the double purpose, not only
of getting rid of the transitory thought, but also of
habituating the mind to rest in the eternal, and to
gain that sense of proportion, that sense that the
present is passing, and therefore is not worth
troubling about; on the side of the permanent, it
will strengthen that dwelling of the mind in the
eternal, which is the secret of all peace in this world,
or in any other.

And as he trains his mind in this way, and as

gradually he gains power over it, and is able to make it think of the thing that he chooses and to refrain from thinking of that which he does not choose, he will take a further step more difficult than either of these, and he will withdraw himself from the mind and think not in the mind at all; not because he is going to become unconscious, but because he is seeking a deeper consciousness; not because the life in him is dulling or becoming lethargic, but because it has become so vivid that the brain is no longer able to contain it; and with this growth of the inner life, with this increase of the life-energy that flows from the Soul, he will slowly find that it is possible to reach a stage where "thought" will no longer be the thought of the mind, but the consciousness in the Soul; long ere he will find that consciousness and realise it, as it were unbrokenly, he will have to pass through the stage of blankness, of emptiness, of void—one of the most trying stages, perchance, of this life of our candidate in the Outer Court; and then he will dimly begin to understand the meaning which is breathed in the words of the Teacher: "Restrain by thy Divine thy lower self; restrain by the Eternal the Divine."* The Divine Self is this Soul which is to restrain the lower mind; but then

* *Voice of the Silence*, p. 47.

beyond the Soul is the Eternal, and, in some future
that lies within the Temple, that Eternal is to
restrain the Divine in him, even as the Divine
restrains the lower self. And then he gradually
and slowly learns that he is to be master of everything that is around him, with which mind-thought
is connected in any way; that he will come to one
of the stages in this Outer Court where subtle
temptations will be flocking around him, temptations that do not touch the lower nature, but that
dare to raise themselves against the higher, and
that strive to use the mind for the destruction of
the disciple, having failed to use the desire-nature
or the grosser temptations of the body. And then
come those subtle temptations that ensnare the
inner man, those thronging crowds of temptations
that come round him as he is rising upwards along
his difficult path, temptations of the thought-world
thronging round him from every side; he must have
gained utter control over the mental images he
himself has created ere he will be able to hold his
own unshaken, serene, unruffled, amid all these hosts
of hurrying thoughts that are now coming to him,
vitalised and strengthened no longer by the feeble
minds of men in the lower world, but with a
tremendous impulse which has in it something of
the nature of the forces of the spiritual plane—from

the dark side and not from the white, from those who would fain slay the Soul, and not from those who would help it. And in the Outer Court he finds himself face to face with these, and they rush on him with the energy that comes from those mighty forces for evil; and if he have not learned and have not trained himself to be master within the limits of the mind against the puny attacks that meet him in the outer world, how then shall he hold his own against these hosts of Mâra, the Evil One? How shall he cross that fourth stage in the Outer Court, round which these enemies of the Soul are clustering, and which refuse that any shall go through who is not absolutely at peace? And then there comes this strength which grows out of the fixity of the mind, the mind which now has grown so strong that it can fix itself on what it will, and stay there unshaken, no matter what whirlwind may be going on around; a fixity so great, so steady, that nothing that is without can avail to shake it at all, which has grown so strong that it does not need effort any longer, that it does not need to slay any more, for it has gone beyond the stage where such effort is necessary; the stronger the Soul, the less of effort in its working; the mightier the power, the less it feels assaults that come to it from without.

Then that great stage of the mind is reached when, instead of being slain, thoughts fall dead of themselves when they reach the shrine; no longer need the mind slay, no longer need itself be slain; it has become cleansed, pure and obedient. And the result of that which is the beginning of the blending of the Mind and of the Soul is that the moment anything alien strikes against it, it falls dead of its own impulsion; there is no longer need to strike, for all that needs to be struck at falls dead by the throwing back of its own blow; and this is that fixity of the mind of which it is written that the lamp is placed in a steady spot where no wind can cause it to flicker. It is in that place of rest where the will is beginning to be realised; it is there that there is absolute peace; it is a spot under the shadow of the Temple walls; and it is of that that it is written in an ancient Scripture that when a man is free from desire, when he is free from grief, it is then in the tranquillity of the senses that he beholds the majesty of the Soul;* then he sees indeed for the first time, no longer by broken gleam, by ray that comes and goes, but in this absolute peace and serenity where there is no desire and no ruffling of grief; there the majesty of the Soul shines out unbroken, and the mind

* *Kathopanishad,* ii., 20.

now a mirror which is polished, reflects it back as it really is. For this mind, that in the early days was a dust-covered mirror, this mind, that was as the lake ruffled by the winds that blow from every side, has become as the polished mirror that reflects perfectly; it has become as the lake which gives back everything in mountain and in sky, the trees to the trees, the stars to the stars, and which has every shade of colour in the heavens, throwing them back again to the heavens whence they come. But how? There is a moment of danger ere this, of which the warning voice has spoken; there is a moment when this spot is almost reached where the lamp will no longer flicker, when the mind and the Soul join for a moment in a last struggle, when the mind becomes as a mad elephant that rages in the jungle; how then shall it be tamed? It is the last struggle of the mind; it is the final effort of the lower to assert itself against the higher, feeling the bonds that are upon it—that rising up of the lower nature of which every book of Initiation has spoken. For it has been written in every book that speaks of the Hidden Wisdom that, as the candidate approaches the gateway, ere he passes into the Temple, all the powers of Nature rise up against him to drag him

down ; every power that is in the world comes out
against him ; it is the last struggle to be passed
through ere the conquest is complete. On higher
planes yet there is a struggle of which this is the
reflection ; on planes so high that we cannot image
them, whereto the greatest of the great have found
their way; and that is symbolised in the last
struggle of the Buddha beneath the Sacred Tree ;
there where came to Him the last illumination that
made Him Buddha, all the hosts gathered round
for the last struggle to see if still His passage could
be blocked ; and though on infinitely lower planes,
there is that crucial struggle also in the life that is
now the life of the disciple, and that is now coming
near the gateway of the Temple.

How shall he conquer in the struggle ? How
shall he on his probationary pathway tread in the
footsteps of those who have gone before ? And
still from the words of the Teacher there comes
the help, still from His lips a hint which shall guide
us : " It needs," we hear spoken in the silence, " it
needs points to draw it towards the Diamond
Soul."* What is the Diamond Soul ? It is the
Soul that has accomplished its union with the true
Self ; it is the Soul without spot or flaw in any part,
translucent—as the diamond is translucent—to the

* *Voice of the Silence,* p. 35.

Light of the LOGOS, which it focuses for men;
the mighty Name that just now I spoke, as I might
speak other Names that really mean the same
although in other tongues, is that of a Soul high
above all others to whom belongs this title of the
Diamond Soul, through which the Light of the
LOGOS Itself shines down to men, shines down
undimmed, so pure is the Diamond, so spotless, so
absolutely flawless is that Soul. It is the Soul to
which we look at the moments of our highest aspiration ; and that which we need to draw us upwards
towards It, is only one glimpse of Its beauty, is
only one touch from Its fire ; for the Soul grows
upwards towards its own as the flower grows
towards the light, and the points that draw it
upwards are these radiant outshinings from the
Diamond Soul, which pour down on that which
is Itself, although so weak and hesitating, and draw
it upwards with Divine strength to union with Itself.
And as the disciple begins to understand, there
grows upon him what is meant by the Diamond
Soul ; he realises that in himself also that Diamond
Soul is to be re-incarnate—" Look inwards! Thou
art Buddha !"—that this mind of his, like this body
of his, is but an instrument for Its service, and is
only useful and precious as it makes music worthy
to reach the higher. And then by devotion these

strings of the mind are tuned, are utterly subdued
to the Soul; the Soul tunes them by the power of
devotion, and then it becomes an instrument of
music fit for the Master's touch; then it becomes an
instrument of music from which all melodies in
heaven and in earth may sound; and at last the
disciple stands before the gateway and realises that
what has happened is this: that he himself has
found Himself; that the Soul that is Himself is
looking upwards to One yet higher with whom
it is now going to blend and to become one; the
further union takes place only within the Temple;
standing at the gateway he has only united Himself
eternal to his self that was perishable—Himself the
Soul to himself that was mind. And then he begins
the worship which means identification with the
highest; then he learns that in his daily life the
Soul can always be worshipping, no matter what the
mind may do, and in what the body may be active;
he realises at last that the life of the disciple is
absolutely unbroken worship of the Highest, contemplation that never ceases of the Diamond Soul,
contemplation of the Supreme which knows no
break; that while the Soul is ever thus busied in
the Court of the Temple, the body and the mind
will be at work for the humanity that needs them,
in the Outer Court, and beyond it in the world;

that this body can be ever active working for men, that this mind may be ever busy working for men ; they are instruments while the man is living, they are his messengers and his workers while himself is worshipping. And then he realises what it means that "in heaven their Angels always behold the face of the Father," for the vision of the Father-Soul is an unbroken vision, no cloud of earth may dim it, no work on earth may mar it ; ever the Soul is beholding, while the mind and the body are labouring, and when that is achieved the threshold is being crossed, and from the Outer Court the Soul is entering into the Temple of its Lord.

LECTURE III.

BUILDING OF CHARACTER.

IN beginning this third lecture of the course, I want as a preliminary step to repeat the warning that I gave you in the first lecture, with regard to the qualifications with which I am dealing, and the line of thought and of action which will be followed by those who are in the position that I have called " In the Outer Court." You will remember that I said to you that the position of an aspirant who had reached that Court was very different from the position even of the good and virtuous and religious man, who had not thoroughly seen the goal which was before him, who had not thoroughly realised the magnitude of his task. And I want again to remind you that in the whole of this, in which I am sketching the qualifications of those who come into the Court, I am dealing with everything from this standpoint of a deliberate self-training towards an aim that is definitely recognised; and more than that, that I by no means mean in speaking of these

F

qualifications that they are completely achieved while the aspirant still remains in the Outer Court of the Temple. He begins, as it were, the making of the character, he realises to some extent what he ought to be, and he strives more or less effectively to become that which he aspires to achieve. It is not that the definite purification, or the complete control of the thoughts, or the perfect building of the character, or the entire transmutation of the lower into the higher—it is not that all these must be accomplished ere he can stand on the threshold of the Temple ; he is really employed whilst in the Outer Court in drawing as it were the foundations of his buildings, in sketching out carefully and fairly fully the outlines of that edifice which he hopes to carry to perfection. The working out of all these lines, the building on this foundation, the raising of the walls higher and higher, the placing of the crowning stone finally upon the work—that is done rather within the Temple than without it, after the eyes have been opened, not while they are still partially blinded and the aspirant is in the Outer Court. But what I do want you to understand is that the plan is sketched, that the plan is recognised ; that nothing less than this—very much more may come in the course of the ages—that nothing less than this is the goal that the candidate sets before himself for the reaching; so that however great may seem the aspirations, however magnificent may seem the outline which is to be filled in, that outline is to be definitely recognised in the Outer Court, although not to be filled in in detail, and however lowly may be the achievements of the present they are none the less the definite foundations on which the glorious achievements of the future are to be based. And I say this thus explicitly, although it be a repetition, because it was suggested to me that in making so wide a scope for the Outer Court, in tracing so vast an outline, it might come on some of my hearers with a sense of discouragement if not of despair; so that it is well that all should understand that while the beginnings are traced they may still be only the beginnings, and that after the threshold is crossed, there are still many lives in front in which these beginnings may be carried to fulfilment, and this plan of the architect serves as basis for the finished edifice. Taking then that as a thing to be understood, let me remind you of the building of the character, which is to be a distinct and a positive building which this candidate in the Outer Court will set before himself; we have seen already that he is to have been in past lives a virtuous and a religious man, that is, that he will have already realised that nothing of absolute vice must have its place in him, that nothing of evil must be permitted to remain; that if any seed of vice remain, it must at once be flung without, that if any tendencies towards positive evil are still there, they must be completely and entirely rooted out. Here in this Court there can be at least no compromise with evil, here there can be at least no paltering with that which is not right and pure and good. While there may still be failures in the achievement of the right, there is most definitely no contented remaining in the wrong; *that* has had the back of the aspirant definitely turned upon it, and all the grosser part of the nature will already have been eliminated, all the rougher part of the inner struggle will have been finished. Into the Court of the Temple utterly unhewn stones cannot be brought for the building; the hewing must have been going on during many previous lives, much work must have been done upon the characters before they become fit to be built at all even in the Outer Court of such a Temple. And this rough-hewing of the character is supposed to lie behind us; we are dealing with the building of the positive virtues, and virtues of an exceedingly high and noble type; virtues which are not those simply that are recognised as necessary in the world, but far rather those which the aspirant desires to achieve in order that he may become one of the Helpers and the Saviours of the world, those characteristics that go to make up one of the world's Redeemers, one of the pioneers of the first-fruits of mankind.

The first thing perhaps that will strike us, in this building of character by one who is in the Outer Court, is its exceedingly deliberate nature. It is not a thing of fits and starts, it is not a casual building and leaving off, it is not an effort in this direction one day and in another direction to-morrow, it is not a running about seeking for aims, it is not a turning about looking for a purpose; the whole of this at least is definitely done, the purpose is recognised and the aim is known. And the building is a deliberate building, as by one who knows that he has time, and that nothing in Nature can be lost; a deliberate building which begins with the materials ready to hand, which begins with the character as it is recognised to exist, which looks, as we shall see, quietly at all its strength and at all its weaknesses, and sets to work to improve the one and to remedy the other; a deliberate building towards a definite aim, a carving in permanent material of a statue of which the mould has already been made.

And so the first thing that will be noticed in these
candidates in the Outer Court is this definiteness of
purpose and this deliberateness of action. The
man knows that he will carry everything on that
he makes; that from life to life he will take with
him the treasures that he has accumulated; that if
he finds a deficiency and only partly fills it up, still
it is filled up to that extent, that part of the work
is done; that if he makes for himself a power, that
power is his for evermore, a part of the Soul never
to be taken away from it, woven into the texture
of the individual, not again ever to be separated
from him. And he builds with this deliberate
purpose which has its root in knowledge, recognising
the Law that underlies every aspect of Nature.
Realising that that Law is changeless, knowing that
he may trust it with uttermost and completest faith,
he calls upon the Law and knows that the Law
will answer, he appeals to the Law and is confident
that the Law will judge. There is in him then
no trace of wavering, no shadow of doubting; he
gives out that which must needs bring to him his
harvest, and every seed that he sows, he sows with
this absolute certainty that the seed will bear fruit
after its kind, that that and none other will come
back to him in future days. So there is naught of
hurry in his work, naught of impatience in his

labour; if the fruit be not ripe, he can wait for the gathering; if the seeds be not ready, he can wait for the growing. He knows that this Law to which he has given himself is at once changeless and good; that the Law will bring all in its appointed time, and that the appointed time is best for him and for the world. And so, as I said, he starts with his available material, content with it because it is what the Law brings him from his past; content with it because it is that with which he has to work, that and nothing else; and whether full or scanty, whether poor and small or rich and great, he takes it and begins to work with it, knowing that however scanty it be there is no limit to the wealth to which it may be increased, and knowing that however small it may bulk to-day, there is no limit to the vastness to which it may grow in the years which lie in front. He knows that he *must* succeed; not a question of possibility but of certitude, not a question of chance but of definite reality. The Law must give back the equivalent of that which he gives, and even if he give but little, that little will come back to him, and from that he will build in the future, adding always something to the store, standing a little higher with each achievement, with each new accomplishment.

Already we know something of the way in which
he will build ; we know that he will begin with right
thought ; and we studied last week this control of
the thoughts, which is necessary in order that the
right may be chosen, and the wrong may be
rejected ; working steadily at that thought control
and knowing its conditions, understanding the laws
by which thoughts are generated and by which
thoughts act in the world and react upon their
generator, he is now in a condition definitely to
choose right thought for the building of his
character. And this stage of right thinking will be
one of the early steps that he will take while he is
traversing the Outer Court. First of all because
his right thinking affects others—and all those who
are thus candidates for the Temple have their
primary motive in the service of others—so that,
in the choosing of his thought, in the selection of
the thoughts that he either generates or permits to
come within his consciousness, his first motive for
such choice will be the effect that these thoughts
will have upon others, not in the first place the effect
they will have upon himself ; far above and beyond
all else he is qualifying for service, and therefore
as he chooses the thoughts to which he will bend his
energy, he calculates their action on the outer
world—how far they will work for helping, how far

they will work for strengthening, how far they will work for purifying; and into the great stream of thoughts that he knows must go out from his consciousness, understanding how that stream is working, he will send the thoughts that are useful to others, with the deliberate purpose of this serving, with the deliberate object of this helping of the world.

And next he will consider the nature of the thoughts as they affect himself, as they react upon him to make his character, a thing that in a few moments we shall see is of the most vital importance, for here indeed is the instrument by which the character will be built; and not only as they react upon his character, but also as, in making that character, they turn it into a magnet for other thoughts, so that he, acting as a focus for high and noble thoughts—not now, we may hope, for thoughts that are actively injurious—will deliberately make his consciousness a magnet for everything that is good, so that all that is evil may die as it strikes against him, as we saw last week, and all that is good may flow into his consciousness to gain there fresh nourishment, to gain there fresh strength and fresh energy; that the good thoughts of others coming to him may go out with new life-impulse given to them, and that he may act not only as a source of help by the thoughts he generates, but as a channel of helping by the thoughts that he receives, that he revivifies, and that he transmits. And these will go to the making of character, so that at the beginning of the building this right thinking will be one dominant influence in his mind, and he will constantly be watching his thoughts, scrutinising them with the most jealous care, in order that into this sanctuary of the consciousness nothing may come which will offend, for unless this be guarded all else is left open to the enemy. It is the very citadel of the castle ; at the same time it is the gateway through which everything enters in.

And then he will learn in this building of character—perhaps he has already learned—to guard his speech ; for right speech, to begin with, must be true, scrupulously and accurately true, not with the commonplace truthfulness of the world, though that be not a thing to be despised, but of that scrupulous and strict truthfulness which is necessary above all to the student of Occultism— truth of observation, truth of recording, truth of thinking, truth of speaking, truth of acting ; for where there is not this seeking after truth and this strenuous determination to become true, there is no possibility of Occultism which is aught but a danger, there is no possibility of anything but fall, deep and terrible, in proportion to the height to which the student may have climbed. For this quality of truth in the Occultist is at once his guide and his shield; his guide, in that it gives him the insight which enables him to choose the true road from the false, the right-hand path from the left; and his shield, in that only as he is covered with this shield of truth, can all the delusions and the glamours of the planes through which he passes fall harmless. For it is in the practice of truth in thought, in speech, and in act, that there gradually wakes up that spiritual insight which pierces through every veil of illusion, and against which there can be in Nature no possibility of setting up a successful deception. Everywhere veils are spread, everywhere in the world of illusion this deceitfulness of appearances is to be found, until the spiritual insight can pierce through the whole of them with unchanging and direct vision. There is no such thing as the development of spiritual insight, save as truth is followed in the character, as truth is cultivated in the intellect, as truth is developed in the conscience; without this nothing but failure, without this nothing but inevitable blunder and mistake.

The speech first of all, then, will be true, and

next it will be gentle. For truth and gentleness are not in opposition, as too often we are inclined to think, and speech loses nothing of its truth by being perfect in its gentleness and perfect also in its courtesy and its compassion. The more true it is the more gentle it needs must be, for at the very heart of all things is truth and also compassion; therefore the speech that reflects the innermost essence of the Universe can neither causelessly wound any living being, nor be false with the slightest shadow of suspicion. True and gentle then the speech must be, true and gentle and courteous; that is said to be the austerity of speech, the true penance and sacrifice of speech which is offered up by every aspirant. And then out of the right speaking and the right thinking, inevitably must flow right acting; that, as an outcome, must be the result of this flowing forth from the source. For action is only the manifestation of that which is within, and where the thought is pure, where the speech is true and right, there the action must inevitably be noble; out of such sweet source the water can only be sweet in the flowing, out of the heart and the brain that have been purified necessarily the action must be right and good. And that is the three-fold cord by which the aspirant is bound alike to humanity and to his Master; the three-fold cord which, in some great religions, stands as type of this perfect self-control; self-control in thought, in speech, and in action—that is the triple cord which binds the man to service that is perfect in its character, which binds the disciple to the Feet of his Master ; the three-fold cord which may not easily be broken.

When all this is realised, and the beginning of it attempted, this candidate of ours will begin a very definite method of practice in his building of the character, and first he will form what is called an " Ideal ". Let us have clearly in the mind what we mean when we use the word " Ideal." The mind working within itself builds an internal image, which is made as the mind grows in strength out of much that it draws from the outer world ; but although it draws the materials from the outer world, the idea is the result of the internal action of the mind upon the materials. An idea is at its highest an abstract thing, and if we realise how the abstract idea is formed in the mere brain-consciousness, we shall then have a very clear view of what is meant by an ideal ; a little enlargement of the idea will give us exactly what we require. Let me take the ancient illustration, an abstract idea of a triangle. The idea of a triangle may be gained at first by the brain-consciousness working in the child through a study of many forms which he is told are triangles. He will notice that they are of many different shapes, that they are made up of lines which go in very different directions. He will find—when he looks at them separately and with this brain-consciousness of the child—he will find them exceedingly different, so that looking at them at first he will see them as many figures, and will not recognise certain underlying unities which give them all the same name. But as he goes onward in his thinking he will gradually learn that there are certain definite conceptions which underlie this one conception of the triangle; that it always has three lines and no more; that it always has three angles and no more; that these three angles put together have always a certain definite value, and that the three lines, called the sides of the triangle, bear certain relations to each other, and so on. All these different conceptions he will gain as he studies, and the mind, working upon the whole of these, extracts from them what is called an abstract idea of a triangle, which has no particular size, and no particular shape, and no particular angles taken separately. And this abstract idea is made up by the working of the mind on all the many concrete forms, so far as the brain-consciousness is concerned. What greater idea this may be the reflection of, I

am not now considering; but it is thus that in the
brain what is called an abstract idea is built, which
has neither colour nor shape nor any special
characteristic of any one form, and which unites
within itself that which makes the many forms of
it a unity. And so when we build an ideal it is an
idea of this abstract kind, it is the work of the
image-building faculty of the mind, which draws out
the essence of all the different ideas that it has
gained of great virtues—of that which is beautiful,
of that which is true, of that which is harmonious,
of that which is compassionate, of that which is in
every sense satisfying to the aspirations of the mind,
of the heart. From all these different ideas, as
they have been seen limited in manifestation, the
essence is extracted, and then the mind constructs
and throws outwards a vast heroic figure in which
everything is carried to perfection; in which
everything touches its highest and most complete
expression; in which we no longer deal with the
things that are true, but with truth; no longer with
the things which are beautiful, but with beauty; no
longer with the things that are strong, but with
strength; no longer with the things that are tender,
but with tenderness; no longer with the beings who
are loving, but with love; and this perfect figure—
mighty and harmonious in all its proportions,

grander than anything we have seen, only not grander than that which in rare moments of inspiration the Spirit has cast downwards into the mind— that ideal of perfection it is which the aspirant makes for himself as perfect as he is able to conceive it, knowing all the time that his most perfect dreaming is but the faintest shadow of the reality whence this reflection has come. For in the world of the Real, there exists in living light that which down here he sees, as it were, in faint reflection of colour, hanging high in the heavens over the snowy mountains of human aspiration; it is still only the shadow of the Reality whence it has been reflected, all that the human soul may image of the perfect, of the sublime, of the ultimate All that we seek. This ideal he forms is still imperfect, for it must needs be so! But, however imperfect it may be, none the less for him it is the ideal according to which his character is to be built.

But why make an ideal? Those of you who have gone so far with me in the working of thought will know why an ideal is necessary. Let me take two sentences, one from a great Hindu scripture and the other from a Christian, to show you how Initiates speak of the same facts, no matter in what tongue they talk, no matter to what civilisation their words may be addressed. It is written in one of the most mystical of the Upanishads, the *Chhándogya* : "Man is a creature of reflection : what he reflects upon, that he becomes ; therefore reflect upon Brahman."* And many thousand years afterwards another great Teacher, one of the builders of Christianity, wrote exactly the same thought put into other words : "But we all, with open face beholding as in a glass the glory of the Lord, are changed into the same image from glory to glory."† Beholding as in a glass : for the mind is a mirror and images are cast upon it and are reflected, and the Soul that in the mirror of the mind beholds the glory of the Lord is changed into that same image from glory to glory. So that whether you take the Hindu speaker or the Christian, whether you read the scripture of the Indian or the scripture of the Western Sage, still the same teaching of the Brotherhood comes out to you—that you must have the ideal before you in order that you may reflect it, and that that on which the mind is constantly dwelling will inevitably be that which the man shall become.

And how shall the building towards the ideal be made ? For that is the question that we must now consider. By contemplation : definitely, with full purpose, choosing his time and not permitting him-

* *Op. cit.*, III. xiv. 1.   † 2 Cor. iii. 18.

G

self to be shaken from it, this aspirant who is
disciplining his own character will contemplate day
by day the ideal that he has builded. He will fix
his mind upon it, and constantly reflect it in his
consciousness. Day by day he will go over its
outline, day by day he will dwell upon it in thought,
and, as he contemplates, inevitably within him will
rise up that reverence and that awe which are
worship, the great transforming power by which
the man becomes that which he adores, and this
contemplation will essentially be the contemplation
of reverence and of aspiration. And as he
contemplates, the rays of the Divine Ideal will shine
down upon him, and the aspiration upwards will
open the windows of the Soul to receive them ; so
that they shall illuminate him from within, and then
cast a light without, the ideal shining ever above
and within him, and marking out the path along
which his feet must tread. And in order that he
may thus contemplate, he must train himself in
concentration ; the mind is not to be scattered, as
our minds so often are. We have to learn to fix it,
and to fix it steadily, and this is a thing that we
should be working at continually, working at in all
the common things of life, doing one thing
at a time until the mind answers obediently
to the impulse, and doing it with the con-

centrated energy which bends the whole mind towards a single point. No matter that many things that you have to do are trivial; it is the way of doing them, and not the things that are done, that makes the training which results in discipleship—not the particular kind of work that you have to do in the world, but the way that you do it, the mind that you bring to it, the forces with which you execute it, the training that you gain from it. And it matters not what the life may be, that life will serve for the purpose of the training; for however trivial may be the particular work in which you are engaged at the moment, you can use it as a training-ground for the mind, and by your concentration you may be making your mind one-pointed, no matter what for the moment may be the point to which it is directed. For remember, when once you have gained the faculty, then you can choose the object; when once the mind is definitely in your hand, so that you can turn it hither and thither as you will, then you can choose for yourself the end to which it shall be directed. But you may just as well practise and gain the control in little things as in great; in fact, very much better, because the little things are around us every day, whereas the great things come but seldom. When the great thing comes, the whole mind arouses itself to meet it; when the great thing comes, the whole attention is fixed upon it; when the great thing comes, every energy is called to play upon it, so that you may bear yourself well when the mighty task is to be accomplished. But the real value of the Soul is tested more in the little things where there is nothing to arouse attention, nothing in any sense to gain applause, where the man is deliberately working for the end that he has chosen, and is using everything around him in order that he may discipline himself. That self-discipline is the key of the whole. Guide your life by some plan; make to yourself certain rules into which your life shall flow; and when you have made them, keep to them, and alter them only as deliberately as at first you formed them. Take so simple a thing— for the body has to be brought under control—take so simple a thing as a definite rule of rising in the morning; fix the time that you feel is best for your work, for your place in your household, and when you have fixed it, keep to it. Do not permit the body at the moment to choose its own time, but train it in that instant and automatic obedience which makes it a useful servant of the mind. And if you find after practising for some time that you have chosen badly, then change; do not be rigid because you are striving to strengthen your will; be ready to change what does not work well; but change it at your own time and with perfect deliberation; do not change it because on the impulse of the moment passion or bodily desire or emotion may be ruling; do not change it at the demand of the lower nature that has to be disciplined, but change it if you find that you have badly chosen. For never in ruling your own life must you make your rule a hindrance to those around you, or choose ways of self-discipline that aggravate or interrupt others instead of simply training yourself.

The next stage, when all this has been clearly recognised as the way in which the character is to be builded, will be to study the character itself; for you are to work with knowledge and not blindly. You will perhaps, if you are wise, in judging your character, take some of the things that great men have put before you as outlining a character which will lead you to the Gate of the Temple. You might take, for instance, such a tracing as is given in the sixteenth discourse in the *Bhagavad Gîtâ* by Shri Krishna to Arjuna, where he is telling Arjuna what should be the qualities which build up the divine character. You might take that as showing you the qualities at which you should aim in building yourself, and as marking out for you that which you desire gradually to evolve. And if you take it as it is sketched in the sixteenth discourse, you find a list of qualities, every one of which might well serve as part of your constant thought and endeavour, remembering that the character is built first by the contemplation of the virtue, and then by the working out of that virtue which has become part of the thought into the speech and the action of daily life. And the list runs—however great it is, we have time enough before us to fill it in— "Fearlessness, Purity of Heart, Steadfastness in the Yoga of Wisdom, Almsgiving, Self-restraint and Sacrifice, and Study of the Shâstras, Austerity and Straightforwardness, Harmlessness, Truth, Absence of Wrath, Renunciation, Peacefulness, Absence of Calumny, Compassion to Living Beings, Uncovetousness, Mildness, Modesty, Absence of Fickleness, Boldness, Forgiveness, Fortitude, Uprightness, Amity, Absence of Pride—these become his who is born with the divine qualities." Not are his at once, but become his, and are made in the building of the character. And you will find, if you read these at your leisure and with care, that you can group them together under very definite heads, and that each of these may be practised, at first of course very imperfectly but still steadily, and day by day—with never a feeling of discouragement at the lack of achievement, but only with joy in recognition of the goal, and knowing that each step is a step towards an end which shall be achieved. And notice how through them run the golden threads of unselfishness, of love, of harmlessness ; see how courage and strength and endurance find also their place, so that you get an exquisite balance of character, a character that is at once strong and tender, that is at once self-reliant and compassionate, that is at once a helper of the weak and in itself strong and unmoved, that is full of devotion and full of harmlessness, that is full of self-discipline and therefore of harmony. Let us suppose you accept that to some extent as an ideal for the guidance of daily thinking, and you begin to work it out ; let us consider a point that is often found in connection with this effort, which is often found in summing up many virtues together, and which is much misunderstood ; pausing a moment upon it, let us see how the building of character towards this virtue will be carried on. It is a name which is strange in English ears : it is indifference ; and sometimes it is worked out in detail as indifference to pleasure and pain, indifference to cold and heat, indifference to blame and applause, indifference to desire and aversion, and so on; what does it really mean ?

First of all, it means that sense of proportion which must come into the life of one who has gained a glimpse of the Real amid the fleeting, of the permanent amid the transitory; for when once the greatness of the goal has been recognised, when once the numberless lives have been realised, when once the aspirant has understood all the length of time that lies in front of him, all the vastness of the task that he is going to achieve, all the grandeur of the possibilities that lie still unveiled before him; when he has caught some glimpse of the Real, then all the things of one fleeting life must take their place in proportion to the whole. And when a trouble comes, that trouble will no longer bulk so largely as it did when one life was all that he realised, for he will begin to understand that he has been through many troubles before, and has come out the stronger and the more peaceful for the passage. And when joy comes, he will know that he has been through many joys before, and has learned their lessons also, and has found amid other things that they are transitory; and so when a joy comes or a pain, he will take it, not failing to feel it, feeling it really far more keenly than the ordinary man of the world can feel, but feeling it in its true place and at its true worth, and giving it only its real value in the great scheme of life. So that as he grows in this indifference, it is not that he becomes less capable of feeling, for he is ever becoming more sensitive to every thrill of the world within and of the world without—inasmuch as he has become more harmonious with the All, he must become more responsive to every shade of harmony that is therein—but that none of these may avail to shake him, that none of these may avail to change him, that none of these may touch his serenity, that none of these may cast a shadow on his calm. For he himself is rooted where storms are not, he himself is grounded where changes have no place, and while he may feel, he can never be altered by them; they take their right place in life, they bear their proper proportion to the whole span of existence of the Soul. That indifference, that true and real indifference which means strength, how shall that develop?

First, by this daily thinking on what it means, and working it out bit by bit until you thoroughly understand it, and working out detail after detail, so that you know exactly what you mean by it. And then when you go out into the world of men, by practising it in your daily life; practising, not by hardening yourself but by making yourself responsive, not by making round yourself a shell that throws everything off, but by making yourself answer to everything that comes from without; at the same time keeping an inner balance which refuses to vary while the change is felt right through. A hard and a difficult lesson, but a lesson that has so much in it of hope and of joy and of keener and more vivid life, that if that were all it were worth while to practise it. For, as the Soul feels itself growing too strong to be shaken, and yet feels every thrill that comes from without, it has a sense of wider life, it has a sense of fuller harmony, it has a sense of ever-increasing consciousness, of ever-growing oneness with that of which it is part. And as the feeling of isolation gradually melts away there flows into it the joy which dwells at the heart of things, and even that which to the ordinary man is painful loses to the disciple its quality of pain ; for he feels it, as it were, as part of the Universal Life, as a syllable which is spoken out of this vast language of Manifestation, and he can learn its meaning without any agony at his own heart, for the peace which grows out of this widening knowledge far overbears to him, and changes as it were his attitude towards everything in the outer world which men know as pain and loss. Thus thinking and thus practising, you will find

this sense grow within you, this sense of calm and
of strength and of serenity, so that you will feel as
though you were in a place of peace, no matter
what the storm in the outer world, and you will
see and feel the storm and yet not be shaken by it.
This peace is the first-fruits of the Spiritual Life,
which shows itself first in this sense of peace and
then in that of joy, and makes the life of the disciple
a growth which is ever upwards and inwards to the
heart which is Love. And out of this there grows
the sense of self-control, that the Self within is
stronger than the changes without, and while it is
willing to respond, it refuses to be altered by the
contacts from without. And then from the self-
control and from the indifference there comes that
power of hating none, on which so much stress is
laid in all the building of character laid down for
the aspirant who would become the disciple.
Nothing is to be hated, everything is to be brought
within the circle of Love, no matter how outwardly
repulsive, no matter how outwardly antagonistic, no
matter how outwardly repugnant; the heart of all
is Life and Love, and therefore this aspirant who
is learning his lessons can shut nothing out from
the circle of compassion; everything is taken within
it according to its own power of feeling, and he is
the friend of every living thing, the lover of all that
lives and feels.

And as he is thus building these stones into his character he becomes fearless; fearless, because hating nothing there is nothing that has power to harm. Injury from without is but the reaction of aggression from within; because we are the enemies of others they in their turn are our enemies, and because we go out into the world as injurers, therefore living things injure us in turn. We, who ought to be the lovers of all living things, go out as destroyers, as tyrants, as haters, grasping the world for tyranny and not for education, as though man's work here were not to educate his younger brethren and lead them upwards by all tenderness and all compassion; we go out and we tyrannise over others, whether they be human or brute, so long as they are weaker than ourselves; and by their weakness we too often measure our tyranny, and by their helplessness too often the burden that we lay upon them. And then we wonder that living things fly from us—that as we go out into the world we are met with dread from the weak, and with hatred from the strong; and we know not in our blindness that all the hatred from the outer world is the reflection of the evil that is in ourselves, and that to the heart of love there is nothing that is hateful, and therefore nothing that can injure. The man that has love can walk unharmed through

the jungle, can walk untouched through the cave of
the carnivorous brute, or take in his hands the
serpent; for there is nothing that has message of
hate to the heart that has in it only love, and the
love that radiates to the world around us, that
draws all things in to serve and not to injure, draws
all things in to love and not to hate. And so at the
feet of the Yogî the tiger will roll in friendship,
and so to the feet of the saint the wildest will bring
their young for shelter and for helping, and all
living things will come to the man who loves, for
they are all the offspring of the Divine, and the
Divine is Love, and when that is made perfect in
man it draws all things inwards to itself. So then
we learn gradually and slowly to walk fearlessly
in the world, fearlessly even though things may still
injure; for we know if we are hurt that we are
only paying the debt of an evil past, and that for
every debt that is paid there is less against us, as it
were, in the account book of Nature. And fearless
too, because we learn to know, and fear springs
from doubt as well as from hatred; the man who
knows has passed beyond doubt, and walks with
foot unfearing where it may tread, for it treads
on solid ground alone, and there are no pitfalls in
its way. And out of this grows a firm and unshaken
will, a will that is based on knowledge, and a will

that grows confident through love. And as the aspirant is crossing the Court of the Outer Temple, his step becomes firmer, and his course becomes more direct, unshaken in its purpose and growing in its strength ; his character begins to show itself out in definite outline, clear, distinct, and firm, the Soul growing onwards to maturity.

And then comes the absence of desire, the gradual getting rid of all those desires that tie us to the lower world, the gradual working out of all those longings which in the lives that lie behind us we found had no satisfaction for the Soul, the gradual casting aside of all the fetters that tie us down to earth, the gradual elimination of the personal desire, and the self-identification with the whole. For this one who is growing is not going to be tied to rebirth by any bonds that belong to the earth ; men come back to the earth because they are held there, tied by these links of desire that bind them to the wheel of births and of deaths ; but this man we are studying is going to be free ; this man who is going to be free must break these links of desire for himself ; there is only one thing that will bind him, only one thing that will draw him back to birth, and that is the love of his fellows, the desire of service. He is not bound to the wheel, for he is free, but he may come back and turn the wheel once more for the sake of those who still are bound upon it, and whom he will stand beside until the bonds of all Souls are broken. In his freeing he breaks the bonds of compulsion, and so he learns a perfect unselfishness, learns that what is good for all is that which he is seeking, and that what serves the All is that which alone he desires to achieve. And then he learns self-reliance; this one who is growing towards the Light, learns to be strong in order that he may help, learns to rely upon the Self which is the Self of all, with which he is growing to identify himself.

There is a thing that he has to face, upon which I must say a word, for it is perchance one of the hardest of his trials while he is working in this Outer Court. When he entered that Court, knowing and seeing the mighty joy beyond, he turned his back on much that makes life glad to his fellows; but there is a time that comes sometimes, there is a time that now and then descends upon the Soul, when, as it were, he has sprung outwards into a void where no hand seems to grasp his own, and where there is darkness around him, and nothing on which his feet may rest. There are times which come in these stages of the Soul's growth when there is nothing left on earth which can satisfy, there is nothing left on earth which can fill, when the friendships of old have lost some of their touch, and the delights of earth have lost all their savour, when the hands in front, though they are holding us, are not yet felt, when the rock beneath our feet, though our feet are planted upon it, is not yet understood as changeless and immovable, when by the veil of illusion the Soul is covered thickly, and it thinks itself forsaken and knows nothing of help that it can find. It is the void into which every aspirant in turn has plunged; it is the void that every disciple has crossed. When it yawns before the Soul, the Soul draws back; when it opens up dark and seemingly bottomless, he who stands upon the brink shrinks back in fear; and yet he need not fear. Plunge onwards into the void, and you shall find it full! Spring forward into the darkness, and you shall find a rock beneath your feet! Let go the hands that hold you back, and mightier Hands in front will clasp your own and draw you onwards, and they are Hands that will never leave you. The earthly grasp will sometimes loosen, the friend's hand will unclasp your own and leave it empty, but the Friends who are on the other side never let go, no matter how the world may change. Go out then boldly into the darkness and into the loneliness, and you shall find the loneliness is the uttermost of delusions, and the darkness is a light which none may lose again in life. That trial, once faced, is found again to be a great delusion; and the disciple who dares to plunge finds himself on the other side.

Thus the building of character goes on, and will go on for lives to come, nobler and nobler as each life is ended, mightier and mightier as each step is taken. These foundations which we have been laying are only the foundations of the building I have hinted at, and if the achievement seem mighty, it is because always in the mind of the architect the building is complete, and even when the ground plan is a-sketching, his imagination sees the completed edifice, and he knows whereto he builds.

And the end? Ah!—the ending of that building of character our tongues not yet can sketch! No paint-brush which is dipped only in earth's dull colours can limn anything of the beauty of that perfect ideal towards which we hope to, nay, towards which we know we shall, eventually rise. Have you ever caught a glimpse of it in silent moments? Have you ever seen a reflection of it when the earth was still and when the heaven was calm? Have you ever had a glimpse of those Divine Faces that live and move—Those that were men and now are more than men, superhuman in Their grandeur; man as he shall be though not as

H

he is, save in the innermost Courts of the Temple?
If you have ever caught a glimpse in your stillest
moments, then you need no words of mine to tell
you; you know of the compassion which at first
seems the whole of the being, so radiant in its
perfection, so glorious in its divinity; the tenderness which is so mighty that it can stoop to the
lowest as well as transcend the highest, which
recognises the feeblest effort, as well as the
mightiest achievement; nay, which is tenderer to
the feeble than to the mighty, because the feeble
most needs the helping of the sympathy which
never changes; the love which only seems not to
be divine because it is so absolutely human, and in
which we realise that man and God are one.   And
then beyond the tenderness, the strength—the
strength that nothing can change, the strength
which has in it the quality of the foundations of the
Universe, on which all worlds might build, and yet it
would not shake, strength so infinite joined with compassion so boundless.   How can these qualities be
in one Being and harmonise with such absolute
perfection?   And then the radiance of the joy—the
joy that has conquered, the joy that would have
all others share its beatitude, the radiant sunshine
that knows no shadow, the glory of the conquest
which tells that all shall win, the joy in the eyes

that see beyond the sorrow, and that even in looking at pain know that the end is peace. Tenderness and strength and joy and uttermost peace—peace without a ruffle, serenity that naught can touch: such is the glimpse which you may have caught of the Divine, such is the glimpse of the ideal that one day we shall become. And if we dare to raise our eyes so high, it is because Their Feet still tread the earth where our feet are treading. They have risen high above us; none the less stand They beside Their brothers, and if they transcend us it is not that They have left us, although on every side They are beyond us; for all humanity dwells in the heart of the Master, and where humanity is, we, its children, may dare to realise we dwell.

LECTURE IV.

SPIRITUAL ALCHEMY.

NOW during the last three lectures we have been considering the stages, carried on as we saw simultaneously, by which the aspirant for entrance into the Temple is gradually purifying himself, is bringing his thoughts under control, is building up his character, or perhaps I should be more accurate in saying, is building its foundations. These are the three stages that we have considered, and we have seen that any one who has thus entered the Outer Court and has set before himself the great task for achievement, will take up these different efforts not so much one after the other, as one beside the other, and will gradually try to bring his whole nature under control, and to direct it towards the achievement of the object which he has set himself to attain.

Let us suppose then, taking these successively, as we are obliged to do for clearness' sake, let us

suppose that our candidate now turns to the consideration of another part of his great task. I have
described this part of it as Spiritual Alchemy; and
I had in mind, in the use of that phrase, a process
of change, a process of transmutation, the allusion
of course being to that work of the alchemist
whereby he changed the baser metal into the nobler,
whereby he changed, say, the copper into the gold.
And I have in my thought a process which goes on
in the world around us, to some extent I should
imagine in the mind and in the life of every
thoughtful and religious person, but which with our
candidate becomes, as I have so often repeated, a
self-conscious and deliberate process, so that he
recognises his method and his end and turns himself deliberately to the achievement of that which
he desires. Now this process of spiritual alchemy
spoken of, may be regarded, I think, in the most
general sense of the term, as a transmutation of
forces. Each man has in himself life and energy
and vigour, power of will and so on; these are the
forces with which he is to work, these are the
energies by which his object is to be attained. By
a process which may fairly be described as
alchemical he transmutes these forces from lower
ends to higher, he transmutes them from gross
energies to energies that are refined and

spiritualised. It is not only that he changes their object, nor is the change of object the point to which my own mind is directed in this phrase; it is rather that he changes and purifies them without as it were altering their essential nature, just as the alchemist, taking this grosser matter, really passed it through a process of purification; not the mere purging away of dross, but a purification that went much farther, that took the very metal itself, that reduced it into a finer and rarer state, and then, as it were, recombined it into a nobler and sublimer type. So that you may imagine the spiritual alchemist as taking all these forces of his nature, recognising them as forces, and therefore as useful and necessary, but deliberately changing, purifying, and refining them. We are concerned with the method of refining, with the way in which this work may be carried out.

The object of this spiritual alchemy is not only this transmutation of the forces, though that is its essential part, but there is a subsidiary side to it which one cannot leave out of account. Souls are bound to earth-life, to the wheel of births and of deaths, by desires; they are held there by ignorance, they are fettered by their longings after material enjoyments, after separated and isolated joys as it were. Continually engaged in actions, these actions bind the Soul, whether they be in themselves good or bad, whether they be in themselves helpful or michievous; none the less as actions they have this characteristic—that action in the ordinary man springs from desire, and that this desire is the binding and the fettering force. Actions must continue to be accomplished as long as man remains in the world; actions are needful to be done else manifestation would no longer be. As a man grows nobler and wiser and stronger, his action becomes an ever more and more important factor in the world's progress. And supposing the greatest should abstain from action, then the progress of the race must necessarily be delayed, its evolution must inevitably be retarded.

How then shall it be possible that action shall be accomplished and yet the Soul be free? How is it possible that action shall be rendered, and yet the Soul shall not thereby be bound and fettered? Here again we shall find a case of spiritual alchemy, whereby the greatest may be the most active in service and yet his service shall touch him not as a liberated Soul, and you have exemplified what seems a paradox—a service which is perfect freedom. Now the phrase "spiritual alchemy" taken as a means to such freedom is only a way of alluding to the fundamental Law of Sacrifice, that

great Law which in the manifested universe lies at
the root of all and is constantly expressing itself,
whose forms are so various that it is easy to mistake
them, whose action is so complicated that it is easy
to blunder. Easiest of all, perhaps, to blunder in
expression; for you are dealing with a many-sided
truth that is seen in many aspects by the minds of
men; that above all has in fact a double aspect as it
is contemplated from above or from below; that is
a Law which permeates the universe, to which every
atom may be said to be subject, and which is, in the
fullest sense of the term, the expression of the
Divine Life in manifestation. In touching such a
Law at all there are endless opportunities for
blundering—blundering on the part of the speaker
in expression, blundering on the part of the hearers
in grasping the thought which is imperfectly given;
so that in dealing with this, one is apt to be one-
sided according to the view which at the moment is
most before the mind; according as the aspect, we
may say, expresses itself on the side of Matter, or
expresses itself on the side of Spirit; according as
we take a standpoint without—looking inwards, or
a standpoint within—looking outwards. In dealing
with a mighty subject where no one word expresses
the thought, and where the grasping of the thought
itself is difficult to those so undeveloped as our-

selves, it is, as I say, most difficult for speaker and for hearer alike to avoid misconception, to avoid laying too much stress on one side or the other, and so losing that even balance from which truth alone can be perfectly expressed. And with regard to the Law of Sacrifice, this perhaps is especially the case.

Let us take it first in its lower aspect, an aspect which must not be overlooked—for it has for us many lessons—but that which is distinctly the lower aspect of it in all the worlds. Let us take it as we find it expressed in manifested Nature, as impressed on the Kosmos, working in the physical, the astral, the mental worlds, and so on ; including a certain relationship between all living things, including a certain relationship not only between living things as we all know them down here, but including other living beings in the worlds which surround us ; and let us stop on this lower aspect for a moment ere we venture to rise towards the higher, for here also we shall find a most useful lesson, a most luminous suggestion for our helping in this process of the Outer Court.

Regarding sacrifice in the lower worlds, it may present itself to us not unfitly as a process of mutual service or exchange, a continual turning of the wheel of life, in which each living being takes and gives, in which he cannot avoid the taking, in which he ought not to refuse the giving. So that you will see sacrifice, if you look at it for a moment in what I have called its lower aspect, as a continual turning of the wheel of life, in which all things take conscious or unconscious part, and the more highly they are developed the more conscious will be their co-operation. This view of sacrifice has been put clearly, perhaps more clearly almost than anywhere else, in *The Lord's Song*, one of the Indian Scriptures, where this wheel of life is dealt with, and where you find sacrifice and action connected in a way which it is well to realise. Says the great Teacher : —

The world is bound by all action, by action with sacrifice for object; with such object, free from attachment, O son of Kuntî, perform thou action.

And then, going backwards into the past in order to make this cycle which is sacrifice by mutual service complete, the Teacher says that : —

Having in ancient times emanated mankind by sacrifice, the Lord of Emanation said : " By this shall ye propagate; be this to you the Kâmaduk (that is, the milk of desire): with this nourish ye the Gods, and may the Gods nourish you ; thus nourishing one another, ye shall reap the supremest good. For, nourished by sacrifice, the Gods shall bestow on you the enjoyment

you desire." A thief verily is he, who enjoyeth what is given by Them, without returning the gift.   . .
From food creatures become ; from rain is the production of food ; rain proceedeth from sacrifice ; sacrifice arises out of action.   Know thou from Brahmâ action groweth and Brahmâ from the Imperishable cometh.   Therefore Brahman, the all-permeating, is ever present in sacrifice. He who on earth doth not follow the wheel thus revolving, sinful of life, and rejoicing in the senses, he, O son of Prithâ, liveth in vain.*

Now you have there this wheel of life which lies at the root of sacrifice in all religions, and the purer and the nobler the religion, the purer and nobler will be the idea of sacrifice which pervades it. Notice how thoroughly there is carried out this alchemical idea, the changing always of one into the other; the food changes into beings, but in order that food might be, the rain had been changed into food ; in order that the rain might fall, sacrifice had been offered to the Gods.   Then the Gods nourish. You will find this turning of the wheel everywhere prominent in these ancient religions. The Brahman, for instance, will cast into the fire his sacrifice, for, it is said, fire, Agni, is the mouth of the Gods ; and the throwing of that sacrifice into the fire in ancient days, accompanied, as it was, with Mantras made by men who knew what they were

* *Bhagavad Gitâ*, iii., 9-16.

making, and made the Mantra as words of power
over the lower forces in Nature, that sacrifice thus
performed regulated many of these forces in
Nature, which working upon the earth bring forth
food for men. Although the action was in itself
a symbol, that which it symbolised was real, and
the force that went forth from the lips of the
purified teacher and the man of power was real also.
The symbol was meant to teach the people about
this wheel of life, to make them understand that
action is essentially sacrifice, and that all action
should be of the nature of sacrifice; that is, that
action should be done as duty, that it should be
done because it is right and with no other object,
that it should be done in order that man may be in
harmony with law, that it should be done because
that is his answer to the law, his part of the common
task. So that under this teaching sacrifice was the
bond of union, the golden thread that linked
together all beings in this manifested universe;
and as the root of sacrifice was action, as action
came from the manifesting God, and as He was
that which manifested, so it was said that Brahman
permeated every sacrifice, and all action that was
done could thus be done as duty in the world, not
with desire for individual fruit, not with desire for
personal gain, not with wish to obtain something

for the personal self—*there* comes in the lower, the debased, the selfish view with which sacrifices were later done. As part of the turning of the wheel, as part of the accomplishment of duty for duty's sake, there is the very essence of the alchemy which, changing action into sacrifice, burns up the bonds of desire, and liberates the wise. Thus burned in the fire of wisdom, action loses all its binding force upon the Soul; the Soul becomes a fellow-worker with the divine in Nature, and every action that is cast upon the altar of duty becomes a force which turns the wheel of life but never binds the Soul.

That, then—this constant exchange, this mutual service—that is one form of the great Law of Sacrifice, and the change which is produced is of this nature, that where the action is done as duty, it becomes part of the universal harmony, distinctly helps forward evolution, distinctly helps in the raising of the race. The work of our aspirant in the Outer Court is gradually to train himself to perform all action in this sacrificial way, realising that he is thus performing it, asking for nothing, seeking for nothing, looking for no fruit, demanding no reward, doing it because it ought to be done, and for no other reason. Who does that, he is indeed performing this work of spiritual alchemy by which all action is purified in the fire of wisdom; he is in conscious harmony with the divine will in the manifested universe, and so becomes a force for evolution, so becomes an energy for progress, and the whole race then benefits by the action which otherwise would only have brought to the sacrificer a personal fruit, which in its turn would have bound his Soul, and limited his potentialities for good. Thus then we may regard this law of sacrifice as working, when regarded in its lower aspect.

Let us come on now to the higher, to the sublimer view, and in order that we may gain this without misconception, I will try to do it the more carefully, and dwell upon it the more fully, because I see how easily mistake may arise out of a partial present-ment, for which I myself am responsible. I want to-night to delay a moment on the essence of sacrifice, and try to realise what sacrifice really means. It seems to me, and this is the thought with which I will ask you to begin, that sacrifice regarded in its innermost essence—regarded from the standpoint in which we shall all regard it more and more as we rise towards the diviner life— sacrifice is a giving or a pouring forth; it is motived by the desire to give, its essence is in the longing to pour forth something which is possessed, and which, being precious to the possessor, he desires to

I

pour out for the helping and joy of others. So that
the way to regard sacrifice, looked at from the
inner side rather than from the outer, is that it is an
act of gift, a pouring forth of the nature for the
purpose of conferring happiness on others, and
therefore it is in its essence joyous and not grievous,
the gift itself being the very heart of the sacrificial
action. Putting aside everything which may take
place for the time in the making of sacrifice—we
will consider that presently—looking at the sacrifice
as sacrifice, it is gift ; and it is offered by a nature
which desires to give, a nature which longs to pour
itself forth, which would fain share with others all
that it has of bliss, and which is motived by this one
longing to pour itself forth into others, so that
they may be one with it in its joy. But, you may
say, why in its joy? Because I asked you to come
back to the very heart and the core of Manifestation.
The supreme act of sacrifice, I ventured to say
elsewhere, was that Self-limitation of the One
Existence by which It put forth as Energy
the manifested LOGOS. I find—not unnaturally,
perhaps, because in dealing with this in its working
out in the universe, I dwelt unduly on one side of
it—that this view of sacrifice has been held to
imply what seems to me a contradiction in terms :
" the agony of the LOGOS." But what is LOGOS?

Brahman in Manifestation; and the nature of Brahman we have been told over and over again in the ancient Scriptures, which in turn have their root in knowledge still more ancient, the nature of Brahman is Bliss. No other thought is possible, if you try to think at all of that which is beyond manifestation. That Brahman is bliss has been the keynote of the most ancient Âryan religion. And as man rises towards Brahman, the very last sheath of the Soul is called the Sheath of Bliss. If you take the Râja Yoga of India, and if you study the vehicles in which the Soul can manifest itself in the worlds, you will find that as it retires from the lower worlds, as it shakes off the lower sheaths, it casts aside the sheath of the body, and then the sheath of the subtle body, and then the sheath of desire, and then the sheath of mind; you will find that as it goes upwards and upwards, ever approaching that Brahman which is itself, and becoming ever more and more its own essential nature, you will find that at the very end there is a sheath, the highest, so subtle that it scarcely differentiates it from the One and Only, the filmy, rare individuality which is necessary in order to keep the whole harvest of the ages which lie behind. And that sheath has a name, and they call it the Sheath of Bliss, as though they would remind every one who is struggling in the world in the coils of ignorance, as though they would remind every one that this progress in Yoga, which is union with the Divine, is to be carriéd on from stage to stage until the Soul is enveloped in nothing but bliss, and then they say: "Brahman is Bliss." So that you realise, if you realise this great teaching at all, that there is not possible an act of sacrifice in that lofty region which can be aught but an act of joy, aught but an act of the giving forth of bliss, and the very essence of the thought—however imperfectly I may have personally expressed the thought matters little —is that from that Supreme Nature which is bliss the universe came forth, from this Self-limiting of Existence came the LOGOS that is Itself. And the very object of the Self-limitation was to pour forth the bliss which was Its own essential nature, so that when the cycle of existence should be completed, there should be many individuals, radiant and joyous, to share with it that perfect bliss, a bliss which should ever grow as they approach to Itself; there is misery only in the supposed distance from It, because of the ignorance in which the Soul is wrapped.

Take then, if you please, that as the essential thought: that the Law of Sacrifice is based on the Divine Nature, that the supreme sacrifice by which

the universe was emanated was this act of giving by
the Nature which is bliss, and that, therefore, the
object of the whole must essentially be this sharing
or scattering of bliss, and that the root of the
sacrifice is this joy in pouring forth to bring many
into union with Itself, of which the end is to be the
Peace which passeth all expression. Realising that,
we shall be able to trace our Law of Sacrifice, and
understand what I spoke of as the dual aspect : the
aspect which in giving, is joy ; but, inasmuch as the
lower nature is a nature which grasps rather than
gives, which shows itself continually from the standpoint of the lower nature as a renouncing, which is
pain. And if we study this a little more closely
I think we shall be able to escape from any
contradiction, and perhaps clarify our eyes when
we are dwelling on this great mystery, as it has well
been called, of the Law of Sacrifice. Let us realise
that giving is the highest joy, because it is of the
essence of the Divine Nature. Let us next realise
that as man becomes himself, that is, as he becomes
in his own self-consciousness divine, he will become
more and more joyful in himself, more and more
joy-giving to others. So that bliss must increase as
the highest nature develops, and pain can arise only
out of the friction in the lower, out of the struggle
of the lower—which is really the Self encumbered

with ignorance and wrapped about with delusions. So that we shall find as we trace this onwards, that the use of pain is to get rid of ignorance ; that the whole process of growth and of evolution is this getting rid of ignorance ; and although that may be described, and is constantly experienced by us in our lower nature, as pain and trouble and conflict, yet in proportion as the true man within us develops, in proportion as he is consciously active, in proportion as he is able to translate himself into the lower nature, just in so far will he realise that the essence of all his efforts is to bring to the helping of a sorrowful world this manifestation of joy and peace ; and he will gradually be able, as it were, to permeate the lower nature with his own conviction, as he gradually purifies it from ignorance and makes it realise the reality instead of the delusive appearance of things.

How then, it may fairly be asked, has this idea of pain been taken so continually in connection with sacrifice ? Why have they been identified so much in thought that the very use of the word sacrifice conveys to the mind of a thinker or a reader the necessary idea of unmingled agony ? It seems as though the root of misconception lay in the lower nature : all its first activities are directed towards grasping, towards taking, towards holding for its own isolated and separated self; coming out into this world for the gathering of experience where the higher man is as yet not at all developed, where his influence over the lower—he himself being so inchoate—is of the slightest possible kind, you will have this lower nature plunging about in the world of sensation, grasping here and there at everything that seems attractive, ignorant of the nature of things, ignorant of the result of things, simply led away by outer appearance, and unknowing of what may lie hidden beneath this delusive surface. So that these early and long-continued experiences of the lower nature will be a constant grasping after apparent delights, and a constant finding that they are less satisfactory than had been imagined; and you may remember that once I worked out for you carefully this meaning and use of pain in its gradual teaching to man of the nature of law, and of the transitory nature of the desires of the senses, of the gratifications of the animal nature. In this way pain leads to knowledge, as also pleasure leads to knowledge; and experiencing these two sides of manifested nature the Soul gathers a little knowledge of the underlying reality of things. Gathering thus the experience which may be, and often is, painful in the gathering, it transmutes its experience into knowledge, changes this knowledge into wisdom, which then it takes as its guide ; as the knowledge accumulates which is held by the real man, this growing self is beginning to realise what it is ; as it transmutes it into wisdom, the wisdom is ever a source of pure and unadulterated joy : This growing wisdom ever means an increasing vision, an increasing serenity, and an increasing strength. So that to it, that which to the lower nature is painful is not unwelcome as bringing with it experience ; where some eagerly grasped gratification is found to bring disappointment and weariness to the true man, he changes that experience into wisdom ; so that from this standpoint even pain has its joyous side, for he sees in the experience not the transitory pain of the lower nature, but the gain of knowledge to the higher, and he realises that all these experiences mean his own growth in knowledge and in power ; he chooses them with a deliberate joy in the choosing, because he sees the end of the working, and the gold that comes out of the fire.

But supposing we take the human being, blinded with ignorance, in the lower world ; suppose we find him learning these lessons which nature is continually teaching, lessons which are stern and painful ; suppose we see him seeking animal gratification, careless of the loss inflicted upon others, careless of the suffering which results to those around him, plunging over others in order to grasp for himself some object of desire; then certainly when he finds it fall to pieces in his grasp, his first feeling will be one of acute pain, of intense disappointment, a sense of weariness and of disgust. And so, looked at from his standpoint, the experience is a truly painful one, although from that higher standpoint it is one that was well worth the gathering because of the wisdom which it brings, the deeper insight into nature, and the surer knowledge of law. But it is far more than that. The lower and the higher find themselves in conflict; the higher wills a certain achievement; through the lower it has to work; the lower understands not the aim of the higher, realises not the object which the higher sees; without that co-operation of the lower the object of the higher cannot be accomplished, and so there is this struggle with the lower nature, sometimes to force it forwards, sometimes to hold it back, and the whole of this, to the lower nature still wrapped in ignorance, results as a feeling of restraint, a feeling of enforced giving up of what it desires to have; but slowly there comes into that lower nature, as the higher works upon it more effectually, an understanding that it is well that this thing should be done, that although there may be pain in the doing, the gain

is well worth the suffering, and that this overcoming
of difficulty by effort, while the effort in itself is
painful, still results in so much gain of strength that
the mere passing pain of the effort is lost in the joy
of the achieving. Thus as the Soul is developed,
there will be, even so far as the lower nature is
concerned, this double working in the intellect, in
the mind of man, in which he will deliberately
choose a thing which is difficult to achieve because
he realises it as supremely desirable ; yet he cannot
gain it without sacrificing some lower desires, and
he sacrifices them and burns them up, as it were, in
the fire of knowledge. He then finds that as he
does it he burns up limitations that held him down,
that he burns up weaknesses that held him back,
and that the touch of the fire, which seemed at first
painful, is really nothing more than the burning of
these chains that held him. Then he joyfully takes
the freedom, and as the experience is repeated, he
realises more and more the freedom, and less and
less the suffering by which the freedom is gained.
So that from that inner standpoint once more this
suffering is changed into joy, for here again is the
divine alchemy, and he sees that in this pouring
forth of the Higher into the lower the Higher is
bringing the lower to share its joy and to feel more
of its permanent and increasing bliss. And when

the Soul is approaching the gateway of the Temple, when this process is to a great extent understood, the Soul will begin to see that all this is really a process of getting rid of limitations, and that the whole of the suffering is in these limitations, which prevent it from realising its oneness with its brothers as well as its oneness with the Divine. As this is understood, and the pouring forth of the Divine Nature, which is the true man, expresses itself, it will constantly be felt that by the bursting of the limitation this diviner joy is found, and that the pain after all is again a question of separation, that the separation has its root in ignorance, and that with the destruction of ignorance there is also the ceasing of pain. And not only that, but as this limitation is felt to be illusory, as this limitation is seen as apparent and not real, and as having no part in the world where the true man is living, then he will begin deliberately to transmute these faculties of the lower nature, and by this alchemical process refine them in the way at which I have hinted in the beginning.

Let us take one or two cases, and see how that might be. Let us take first what is one of the great sources of pain in the lower world—the seeking of pleasure for the personal self, without regard to the

wishes or the feelings of others ; the desire to enjoy
in separation, the desire to enjoy in a little circle
which is fenced from the whole world outside, and
is kept for this limited enjoyment of the lower self.
That pleasure-seeking instinct, as it is sometimes
called, how shall the Soul deal with that ? Has it
anything in it that may be changed in the fire ?
The pleasure-seeking which always ends in suffering may be changed into a joy-spreading faculty,
in which all shall share that which the one has
gained. The Soul finds that it can carry on this
transmutation by gradually seeking to eliminate the
element of separateness from this pleasure-seeking
outgoing, by constantly trying to get rid of this
desire to exclude, by knocking down the little wall
of ignorance raised round itself in these lower
worlds in which it is manifesting, by burning up
that lower wall so that it shall no longer divide
itself from its other selves, so that when a pleasure
is thought of and gained the self pours itself out
amongst all its brethren, and carries to them the
happiness that it has found. But still in truth it
finds joy in seeking obedience ; for in a world
where all is law, harmony with it must always bring
peace and happiness, and the very presence of the
discord is the showing of a disharmony with the
law. But this Soul which is growing, when it finds

that it has gained some spiritual power, when it finds
that it has gained some spiritual knowledge, when it
finds that it has gained some spiritual truth, will
train itself to feel that the joy of possession lies
really in the act of giving, not in the act of gaining,
and that what it needs to do is to break down all
these walls that it once made round itself in the
days of its ignorance, and let the joy spread out
over the whole world of men and of things. And
thus the pleasure-seeking instinct may be transmuted into the joy-giving power, and that which
once sought pleasure in isolation shall realise that
joy is only found in sharing, and that nothing is
worth having save that which is possessed in giving.
And the joy of the giving is really the essential
sacrifice, the pouring out to all of that which
otherwise would become entirely worthless as being
contained within a separated self.

Take another case for this same spiritual alchemy
—the love which is selfish. Now here we have
something higher than a pleasure-seeking instinct;
for the very word love at least implies some giving
to another, else were it not love at all; but it may
still be a very selfish love, a love which is always
seeking to get instead of to give, a love which is
trying how much it can obtain from the objects of
its love, instead of how much it can give to them,

a love which just because it seeks to gain is sure to show forth the unlovely attributes of exclusiveness, of jealousy, of the desire to keep others outside, of the desire to have the beloved object for itself, and as it were to roof in the sun and keep it shining only in its own dwelling, none other benefiting from its rays. But a love that is selfish, how shall it be changed? Not by diminishing the love; that is the blunder that some men make; not by chilling it down and making it colder and harder as it were, if love could ever be cold and hard; but by encouraging the love and deliberately trying to eliminate these elements which degrade it; by watching the lower self, and when it begins to build a little wall of exclusion, knocking that wall down; when it desires to keep that which is so precious and so admirable, then at once trying to share with its neighbour; when it tries to draw the loved one from others, rather to give him out that he may be shared by others. The Soul must realise that what is beautiful and joy-giving should be given to all in order that they too may have the happiness which the one is receiving from the object which is beloved, so that all these grosser elements shall gradually disappear. When the feeling of selfishness arises, it shall deliberately be put aside; when the feeling of jealousy expresses itself, it shall at once be put an end to; so that where the feeling was " Let us keep alone and enjoy," it shall be changed into " Let us go forth into the world together to give and share with others the joy that together we have found." So that by this process of alchemy, the love will become divine compassion, and will spread itself over all the world of men; so that which found its joy in receiving from the beloved, will find its delight in pouring forth to all that which it has found. And this love which once was selfish, which once perhaps was the love between one man and one woman, and then widened out into the circle of the home, and then widened out still further into the life of the community, and then widened out into the life of the nation, and then into the life of the race, shall finally widen out to include everything that lives in a universe where there is naught that lives not; and it shall have lost nothing in its depth, nothing in its warmth, nothing in its intensity, nothing in its fervour, but it shall have spread over the Universe instead of being concentrated on a single heart, and shall have become that ocean of compassion which includes everything which feels and lives. Such would be, with regard to love, this alchemy of the Soul.

And thus you might take quality after quality of

the lower nature, and trace it out as I have traced these two, and you will see that the whole of the process is essentially a getting rid of the separateness, a burning up of that by deliberate will and deliberate knowledge and understanding, and that the whole of the process is a joy to the true, the real man, however much the lower man may sometimes in his blindness fail to understand. And when once that is known, then that which was pain loses its aspect of pain, and becomes a joy, and even in the absolute sensation of what otherwise would have been pain, the joy overbears and changes the suffering, because the Soul sees, and the lower nature begins to understand, the end and the object of the work.

And thus tracing this subject we shall realise that there is yet another way in which this transmutation may occur; that as this fire of wisdom and of love, which is the Divine Nature in man, comes forth into the lower nature more and more, burning up these limitations that I have spoken of, and transmuting it into its own likeness, there is also a liberation of spiritual energy, a liberation of spiritual power; this Self which is thus manifested in the lower man is able to put forth energies and powers which seem in some strange way to be the outcome of the process that we have been tracing, an alchemy in

Nature by which—as this Soul, with its fire of love
and of wisdom, becomes manifest in the world of
men—in the very manifestation it seems to liberate
energy, in the very burning up of the lower it sets
free subtle forces of the higher; so that the result
of the burning is the liberation of the spiritual life,
the setting free of that which was bound and
could not manifest itself, but which, when this outer
film shall be burned up, is freed for work in the
world. We come dimly to understand, as the Soul
is rising on to higher planes, and realising its
identity with all and the oneness of all, we begin
dimly to see the outline of a great truth: that it
is able by virtue of its oneness with other Souls to
share with them and to help them in many ways,
and that it is able to surrender and feel joy in the
surrender of that which it might have had for itself,
but which, having identified itself with all, it must
needs give to the world. And so what might be
called the prize of spiritual achievements—the
possibilities of spiritual rest, and spiritual bliss, and
spiritual growth, which could not be shared with
others—may be surrendered by this Soul as a joyful
act, which is for it a necessity of its own nature,
in order that all it surrenders may become common
property, and spread through the race of men to
help forward their evolution. And so we hear of

K

disciples who give up Devachan, and we hear of
Adepts who give up Nirvâna, and we realise dimly
that what it means is that these are reaching a
point of self-identification with their brothers which
makes it a divine necessity for them to share with
others that which they have gained; that the
true reward for them does not lie in the bliss of
Devachan or in the unimaginable beatitude of
Nirvâna, but that the only joy they care to take is
the throwing of all that is theirs, all that which they
might have enjoyed, into the common stock, thus
helping forward the common evolution, the lifting
upward a little of the race of which they are a part.

And then we catch a glimpse also of another
truth, of the way in which this help may sometimes
be given; and we see that when a man is weighed
down under suffering that he has made for himself,
and when in the great sweep of the law which may
never be broken, there fall upon a human Soul pain
and suffering, of which he himself has been in the
past the sower and the cause—that when that
suffering comes upon him, it is possible for one who
knows no separation, who realises that he and this
suffering Soul are one on the plane of Reality—not
to take the inevitable result upon himself, leaving
him who had sown the seed to escape reaping the
harvest, but—to stand, as it were, beside him in the

reaping, and to breathe strength and energy into
his Soul; thus, while the burden is borne by the one
who made it, and the harvest is reaped by the one
who sowed it, there is still, as it were, thrown into
that Soul a new strength, and a new life, and a new
understanding, which make it possible for him to
fulfil his task, which change not the task but the
attitude of the Soul in the doing it; which change
not the burden but the strength of the Soul which
lifts it; and one of the greatest joys, one of the
highest rewards which can come to the Soul which
is growing, and which is asking nothing for itself
save the power of service, comes, when it sees a
weaker Soul that is being crushed because it is
weak, and finds that it can breathe into that Soul
some breath of divine courage and of relief, and of
the understanding that will give hope and the power
to bear.   The help which is given is the strengthening of the brother-Soul to accomplish; not the
setting free that Soul from a burden which it has
made, and which for its own sake it should bear,
but a breathing into it of that power which grows
out of an understanding of the nature of things, and
which really for it also changes the pain of the
suffered penalty into the quiet endurance of a well-
deserved pain which teaches its own lesson.   A Soul
thus aided becomes joyous even while bearing the

burden of its Karma; and the gift which is given to it is a gift which makes it stronger now and in the future and which is the outpouring of the Divine Life from the plane where all Souls are one; that plane is kept full of this spiritual energy which can help by the constant giving of those who have found the divine joy of pouring themselves out, and who know no phase of reward other than the seeing their brothers rising upwards to the light that they themselves have achieved.

But if this be true, what means the difficult thought with which we are all familiar, which our aspirant most certainly will constantly have heard, which he feels himself to be facing when he enters on these probationary stages, and which he fancies covers all that lies on the other side of the gate into the Outer Court? Why has the Path been called " the Path of Woe," if, as the Path is trodden, it becomes ever more radiant with this diviner joy? Yet it is not hard to understand why that phrase should have been used, if you realise to whom the Path at first must needs seem a Path of Woe; if you understand that in this breasting of the mountain side, in this deliberate will to climb so rapidly, in this deliberate determination to outstrip the ordinary human evolution, one inevitable result of the effort must be the concentration into a few lives of the results that would else have been spread over many, the coming down on the Soul of the Karma of the past, which now has to be faced and to be dealt with in so brief a time, and therefore with a tremendous added force of intensity. When first that falls upon the Soul, it may come with a bewildering force, it may come with a blinding energy, which makes it realise suffering as it has never realised it before. But even then it is not the Soul itself which feels the woe; it is the lower nature, blinded still and ever forced onward by the higher; even in that moment of bitter trial, when all that is accumulated in many a life behind is coming down on the Soul that has dared thus to challenge its destiny, even in that moment the Soul itself is in a place of peace, and is joyous that this should be done speedily which otherwise had lasted through so many lives, and that in a fire which may be keen, but which yet is brief, the dross of the past shall be utterly purged away, and it shall be left free to go onward to the life which alone it recognises as desirable.

Thus it is that this path, looked at from beneath, has been called a Path of Woe, and also because men on entering it give up so much that to the world appears as pleasure—pleasures of the senses, pleasures of the worldly life, enjoyments of every

description, which so many people think and feel
are the very flowers along the pathway of life.
But this Soul that is resolute to climb has lost its
taste for them, this Soul desires them no longer,
this Soul seeks something that does not fade, and
joys that are not transient ; and although the Path
may look from the outside like a Path of Renunciation, it is a renunciation which, on the other side,
means added joy and peace and happiness ; for it
is not the taking of woe for pleasure, but the throwing aside of a passing happiness for eternal bliss,
the giving up of a thing which can be taken from
it by outer circumstances for that which is the
inner possession of the Soul itself, treasures which
no robber can ever touch, joys which no change of
earthly circumstances can dim, or mar, or cloud.
And as the Soul goes onwards along the Path, the
joy deepens and deepens ; for we saw at the
beginning that sorrow had its root in ignorance.
True, the bitter pain will often come before the
knowledge, but that is because of the ignorance,
because of the blindness.   There is sorrow in the
hearts of those who, because of the sorrow perhaps,
give themselves to the seeking of the Path, when they
look over the world of men and see the misery and
the wretchedness on every side, when they see the
suffering of men, of women, and of children coming

back century after century, and millennium after
millennium, when they see men suffer who know
not why they suffer, and so have that sting of
ignorance which is really the essence of pain. In
looking over the world sunk in ignorance, and on
men struggling amidst its coils, then it is that the
hearts of the men who are to be the Saviours of
mankind feel the misery of the world, and this
inspires·them to seek for it the Path of Liberation.
But has it never struck you, looking back to the
history of those great Ones, and catching such
glimpses of their lives as we may from history or
tradition in the world of men, has it never struck
you that this agony that They went through was
before They saw the light? That the agony was
the agony of helplessness, the reflection of the
sorrows that They realised while yet They saw not
the cause, of the sorrow that They felt while yet
They knew not the curing? And if you take the
sorrow of that Divine Man, whom so many millions
of our race to-day regard as highest and greatest,
the very flower of humanity, the Buddha who now
has for lovers one-third of the human race, do you
remember how He sought the cause of sorrow, how
He mourned over the ignorance and the misery of
the world, and saw not—it is said, perchance in
parable, saw not—how that sorrow might be cured;

how He went through suffering and pain and self-
denial, how He renounced wife, and child, and
palace, and home, and kingdom; how He went out
with only the mendicant's bowl alone into the
jungle, far from the haunts of men; and how His
heart was heavy within Him, and His eyes were
clouded? He knew not, it is said, how to save the
the world, and yet He could not be at peace while
the world was suffering; He went through many a
danger, through many a pain, through mortification
of the body, and the denser darkness and misery of
the mind which sought to see but could not; and
at last, sitting beneath the tree, there came
illumination, and He knew the cause of sorrow; and
then there came the time when sorrow vanished and
joy took its place; when, in the words that have
come ringing down through the centuries from His
lips, there is the cry of triumph, of joy, of happiness
that shall know no future change. You may
remember the words in which an English poet has
voiced His saying, which show how the ignorance
was the cause of the sorrow, and how knowledge
was the seeing, and the coming of the joy :—

> I, Buddh, who wept with all my brothers' tears,
> Whose heart was broken with the whole world's woe,
> Laugh and am glad, for there is liberty.

Liberty! but that is joy. The tears came from

ignorance; the tears came from blindness; the heart was broken with the world's woe, as men's hearts are breaking now because they know not. But there is liberty. And the message of liberty is that the cause of sorrow lies in ourselves and not in the universe; that it lies in our ignorance and not in the nature of things; that it lies in our blindness and not in the life. Thus it is that when the light comes, liberty comes with it, and the joy and the laughter, as it is said, of the man become divine. For the divine light has flowed in upon His Soul, He is the illuminated, the wise; and for the wise there is no such thing as sorrow, for the divinely illuminated Soul grief is dead for evermore.

LECTURE V

ON THE THRESHOLD.

TO-NIGHT we stand before the Gates of Gold, those Gates that every man may open—those Gates which, once passed, admit a man into that great ·Temple of which we spoke four weeks ago—that Temple from which he who enters goeth out no more. And we are to try to-night, if we can, to realise something of the state of the aspirant who is thus approaching the threshold, who is hoping soon to pass into the Temple, to join the ranks of those who are set apart for the service of the world, for the helping on of the evolution of the race, for the more rapid progress of humanity. Looking for a moment over the dwellers in this Outer Court, in which we have spent our time during the last four lectures, there is one characteristic which seems to be common to every one who is there. They differ very much in their mental and in their moral

qualities; they differ very much in the progress
that they have made; they differ, as is perceptible
enough as we study them, in the qualifications which
they have already obtained, in their fitness to pass
onwards; but one thing they all seem to have in
common, and that is earnestness. They have a
definite purpose before them. Definitely and
clearly they understand to what they are aspiring,
they are looking on the world with an earnest
purpose under their life; and this, it seems to me,
is perhaps the most salient characteristic and the
one which, as I said, is common to them all. Those
of you who are at all familiar with sacred literature
in other lands than this will remember how much
stress is laid on this quality of earnestness, of a
definite purpose working itself out in a definite way.
If you look at some of the ancient books belonging
to the Indian faiths you will find that heedlessness
is marked as one of the most dangerous of failings;
earnestness, on the other hand, as one of the most
valuable of attainments; it matters not to what
religion you turn, you will find on this a perfect
unanimity. Every one who has reached this stage
that we are thinking of has passed beyond the
bounds that separate one creed from another, has
realised that in all creeds there are the same great
teachings, and that all religious men are seeking

the same great goal; so that it is not surprising that whether you turn to the Scriptures that belong to one faith or another, inasmuch as they all come from the same great Brotherhood of Teachers you will find the same characteristics are noted as marked in the aspirant, and all of them speak of this quality of earnestness as one of the most essential for the would-be disciple. As clearly, perhaps, and a little more in detail than anywhere else, you will find the quality worked out in the second chapter of the *Dhammapada.* It says there :—

If an earnest person has roused himself, if he is not forgetful, if his deeds are pure, if he acts with consideration, if he restrains himself, and lives according to law, then his glory will increase.

By rousing himself, by earnestness, by restraint and control, the wise man may make for himself an island which no flood can overwhelm.

Fools follow after vanity, men of evil wisdom. The wise man keeps earnestness as his best jewel.

Follow not after vanity, nor after the enjoyment of love and lust! He who is earnest and meditative obtains ample joy.

When the learned man drives away vanity by earnestness, he, the wise, climbing the terraced heights of wisdom, looks down upon the fools; serene he looks upon the toiling crowd, as one that stands on a mountain looks down upon them that stand upon the plain.

Earnest among the thoughtless, awake among the

sleepers, the wise man advances like a racer, leaving
behind the hack.

By earnestness did Maghavan rise to the lordship of
the Gods. People praise earnestness; thoughtlessness
is always blamed.

A Bhikshu who delights in earnestness, who looks
with fear on thoughtlessness, moves about like fire,
burning all his fetters, small or large.

In looking back over the whole of the work that
we have been tracing, you may see how this quality
of earnestness underlies the whole purification of
the nature, the control of the thoughts, the building
of the character, the transmutation of the lower
qualities into the higher; the whole of this work
presupposes the earnest nature which has recognised
its object and is definitely seeking its goal.

This then, as I say, may be taken as the common
characteristic of all who are in the Outer Court,
and it may be worth while perhaps to note in
passing, that this characteristic shows itself in a
very salient way to those whose eyes are opened.
You will all of you know that the character of a
person may be very largely read in what is called
the aura that surrounds him; and some of you may
remember that in dealing with the evolution of man,
and taking different points in that evolution, I
have sometimes suggested to you that in the very
early days the Soul is a most indefinite thing; that it

might be, and that it has been, compared to a kind
of wreath of mist with no definiteness of outline,
with no clear limit marked. Now as the Soul
progresses, this mist-wreath assumes a more and
more definite form, and the aura of the person
assumes a correspondingly more and more definite
shape; instead of ending vaguely, shading off into
nothingness, it will take to itself a clear and definite
outline, and the more the individuality is formed,
the more definite this outline will become. If, then,
you were looking at people in the Outer Court, this
would be a characteristic that would be visible :
they would be people whose auras would be well
defined ; not only would they show very definite
qualities, but these would be clearly marked
externally, this clearness of marking in the aura
being the outer sign of the inward definiteness
which the individual Soul is assuming. And I am
saying this in order that you may understand and
realise that this condition of the Soul is a thing that
marks itself as it advances ; it is not a thing where
mistake can arise. The position of the Soul is not
one given to it by arbitrary favour from any one ;
it is not given by any kind of chance, nor does it
depend upon any sort of accident ; it is a clear and
definite condition, showing qualities definitely
achieved, powers definitely gained, and these are

L

marked out clearly, so that they are visible to any observer who has developed within himself the powers of sight beyond those concerned with mere physical matter. The quality of earnestness, then, results in developing the individuality, and in thus giving this clear definiteness to the aura; the definitely outlined atmosphere which surrounds the person may be said to be the external mark of the internal state which is common to all who are in the Outer Court; and although this will be more clearly shown in some than in others, it will be characteristic of every one who is there.

While the aspirants are in the Outer Court, it has been said, and quite truly said, in that wonderful little treatise, *Light on the Path*, that the initiations are those of life; they are not the clear and definite Initiations that come later, not those definite steps which are within the Temple, the first of which comes on the passing through the Golden Gates; but they are constant initiations which come in the way of the candidate as he is going along the path of his daily life, so that in a very real sense life may here be said to be the great Initiator; and all the ordeals through which the candidate is passing here in this life thus prove his strength and develop his faculties. And if you turn to that same little treatise, *Light on the Path*, you will find that certain conditions are there laid down which are said, in the " Comments " afterwards published in *Lucifer*, to be written in every ante-chamber of any Lodge of a real Brotherhood. These rules are said to be written in every ante-chamber, the chamber which comes before the entrance into the Lodge itself.   And those rules are put into language, mystical in its character but still intelligible enough, although indeed, as in all mystical language, difficulties may arise by taking words too literally, in the sense of the mere words rather than as explanation of the inner verities that the words are trying to express.   And those four great truths which are written in the ante-chamber are, you will remember, as follows : —

Before the eyes can see, they must be incapable of tears.

Before the ear can hear, it must have lost its sensitiveness.

Before the voice can speak in the presence of the Masters, it must have lost the power to wound.

Before the soul can stand in the presence of the Masters, its feet must be washed in the blood of the the heart.

Now the same writer through whom *Light on the Path* itself was given was used, as you may remember, a little later to further explain *Light on the Path* by the writing of certain comments,

and these deserve careful study, as they explain
much of the difficulty that may be found by the
student in the treatise itself, and may help him
perhaps to avoid that over-literalness of which I
spoke and to grasp the inner meaning of these four
Truths, instead of being misled by the mere outer
expression. It is said in these that the meaning
of this first phrase, " Before the eyes can see, they
must be incapable of tears," is that the Soul must
pass out of the life of sensation into the life of
knowledge, must pass behind and beyond the place
where it is constantly shaken by these vehement
vibrations that come to it by way of the senses,
must pass out of that into the region of knowledge,
where there is fixity, where there is calm, and where
there is peace; that the eyes are the windows of
the Soul, and those windows of the Soul may be
blurred by the moisture of life, as it is called; that
is, by all the effects of these vivid sensations,
whether of pleasure or of pain, causing a mist to
be thrown upon the windows of the Soul, so that
the Soul cannot see clearly when it looks through
them; a mist which comes from the outer world
and not from within, which comes from the
personality and not from the Soul, which is the
result of mere vivid sensation and not of the understanding of life. It is, therefore, represented by

the name of tears, because these may be taken as the symbol of violent emotion, whether of pain or of pleasure. Until the eyes have grown incapable of such tears, until the windows of the Soul no longer are dimmed by the moisture that can be thrown upon them from without, until these windows are clear and the light of knowledge comes through them, until that has been gained, it is impossible that the eyes of the Soul shall really see. Not, as it is explained, that the disciple will lose his sensitiveness, but that nothing that comes from without will be able to throw him from his balance ; not that he will cease either to suffer or to enjoy, for it is said that he will both suffer and enjoy more keenly than other men, but that neither the suffering nor the joy will be able to shake him in his purpose, will be able to shake him from that point of equilibrium which comes from the steadiness of the knowledge that he has obtained. This knowledge is the understanding of the permanent, and therefore of the incapacity of the transitory and the unreal to throw any definite veil over the vision of the Soul.

And so with the second truth, "Before the ear can hear, it must have lost its sensitiveness." It must have reached the place of silence ; and the reason for this, it is said further, is that though the voice of the Masters be always sounding in the world, men's ears do not hear the voice while they are filled with the sounds of the outer life; it is not that the Master does not speak, for He is speaking ever; it is not that the voice does not sound forth, for it is ever sounding; it is only that the sounds that are immediately around the disciple are so loud, that this sweeter and softer harmony is unable to penetrate to the ear through the grosser sounds that come by the senses and the lower emotions. Therefore it is necessary that silence for a time shall come; therefore it is necessary that while still in the Outer Court the disciple shall reach a place of silence in order that the true sound may be heard; therefore it is that this place of silence which he reaches must for a time give almost the feeling of want of sensitiveness, from the very quiet that is there, from the unbroken stillness of which the Soul is conscious.

And here this same writer speaks, and speaks very strongly, of the difficulty and the struggle which come when first the silence is felt. Accustomed as we are to all the sounds around us, when silence for a moment falls upon the Soul it comes with a sense of nothingness; it is like entering into an abyss in which there is no footing, passing into a darkness which seems like a pall which has fallen on the

Soul—a sense of absolute loneliness, of absolute vacuity, a feeling as though everything had given way, as though all life had vanished with the cessation of the sounds of living things. So that it is said that though the Master Himself be there, and be holding the hand of the disciple, the disciple feels as though his hand were empty; that he has lost sight of the Master and of all that have gone before him, and seems to himself as though poised alone in space, with nothing above or below, or on either hand. And in that moment of silence there seems to be a pause in the life; in that moment of silence everything seems to have stopped, even though it were the very life of the Soul itself. And it is across that silence that the voice sounds from the other side, the voice which once heard in the silence is heard for evermore amidst all sounds; for once heard the ear will respond to it for evermore, and there are no sounds that earth can make thereafter which will be able, even for a moment, to dull the harmony that thus has once spoken to the Soul. And these two Truths, it is said, must be felt, must be experienced, before the real Golden Gate can be touched: these two Truths must be realised by the aspirant, before he can stand on the threshold and there await permission to enter within the Temple itself.

The other two Truths seem, from the description that is given of them, to belong rather to the life that is within the Temple than to that without it, although indeed they be written in the ante-chamber; for much is written in that ante-chamber which is to be worked out on the other side, written for the guidance of the aspirant, that he may know the line along which he is to travel, that he may begin the preparation for the work that lies within the Temple itself. For it would seem from the description as though these other two great Truths —as to the power of speaking in the presence of the Masters, and standing upright before Them face to face—are only realised, in their fulness at least, upon the other side, even though an attempt may be made in the Outer Court to begin to make them flower in the Soul. And the first germs, as it were, may begin to show on the hither side of the Golden Gate; for this power of speaking in the presence of the Master is said to be the appeal to the great Power that is at the head of the Ray to which the aspirant belongs; that it echoes upwards, and then echoes downwards again to the disciple, and from him outward into the world; that it consists in his appeal for knowledge, and the answer to the appeal for knowledge is the giving to him of the power to speak the knowledge that he receives. And the only condition which permits him to speak in Their presence, is that he shall also speak to others of the knowledge that he has gained, and become himself a link in that great chain which joins the Highest to the lowest, handing on to those who stand not where now he stands, the knowledge which, in that place of his standing, he is able to receive. And so it is that it is said that if he demand to become a neophyte, he must at once become a servant, for he may not receive unless he be willing to impart. This power of speech—not power of outer speech which belongs rather to the lower planes, but that power of true speech which speaks from Soul to Soul, and tells the way to those who are seeking it, not by merely outer words, but by conveying to them the truth that the words so imperfectly express—that power of speech from Soul to Soul is given to the neophyte only as he desires to use it for service, as he desires to become one of the tongues of living fire which move amongst the world of men, and tell them of the secret which they are seeking.

Then comes that last Truth that none may stand in the Masters' presence save those whose feet are washed in the blood of the heart. That is explained to mean that just as the tears stand for that moisture of life which comes from vivid sensa-

tion, so does the blood of the heart stand for the
very life itself; that when the blood of the heart
is spoken of, in which the feet of the disciple are
washed, it means that he no longer claims his life
for himself, but is willing to pour it out so that
all the world may share. And inasmuch as the life
is the most precious thing a man has, *that* it is which
he is said to give ere he may stand in the presence
of Those who have given all; no longer has he a
desire of life for himself, no longer seeks he birth for
that which he may gain therein, or that which he
may experience; he has washed his feet in the
blood of the heart, he has given up the desire for
life for himself, and he holds it for the good of the
race, for the serving of humanity; only when thus
he gives all that is his may he stand in Their
presence who have given all. You see then why it
is that I say that those two last Truths seem to
apply rather within the Temple than without it;
for that absolute sacrifice of all life, that breaking
free from all desire, that having nothing save for
the sake of giving, that is in its last perfection
the achievement of the very highest of those who
stand on the threshold of Adeptship; that is one of
the last triumphs of the Arhat, who stands just
beneath that point where all knowledge is achieved,
and there is naught more to learn, naught more to

gain. But still the knowledge that such is the truth which is to become a living reality, is a help in the guiding of the life, and therefore I presume it is written in the ante-chamber, although there be none in that ante-chamber who may hope perfectly to attain to it.

Taking then these stages which lead us to the threshold, we begin to realise something of what they will be who are ready to stand at the Gate, ready to cross the threshold; still with much of imperfection, still with much that remains to do, still with lives in front of them in which much is to be achieved, still with four great stages to be passed through ere yet they reach the lofty position of the Adept. We see that they are people of definite purpose, of definite character, of purified lives, of extinguished or extinguishing passions, of self-controlled character, of longing desire for service, of aspirations towards purity, of the highest nobility of life. Dare we for a moment stand on the threshold itself, glancing forward, if only for a moment, in order that we may realise still more clearly what lies in front, and so understand also more clearly why such conditions are made, and why in the Outer Court the aspirant must practise the lessons we have been studying? Just for a moment let our eyes rest, though they can rest but imperfectly, on the four Paths, or the four stages of the one Path, that lie within the Temple, each with its own Portal, and each Portal one of the great Initiations. The first, that which you will find so often described as the Initiation which is taken by him who " enters on the stream "—that you read of in *The Voice of the Silence* and elsewhere in many exoteric books—which marks as it were a passage, a step definite and clear, which makes the passage over the threshold into the Temple, from which, as I was quoting just now, no one who has once entered ever again goes forth, returning backwards into the world. He goes not forth, for he is ever in the Temple even when he is serving in the world itself.

That entering of the stream, then, is a definite step, and you will sometimes see it said in the exoteric books that there may be seven lives, and often are seven lives, that lie in front of the candidate who thus has entered the stream. In a note of *The Voice of the Silence* it is said that it is very rarely that a Chela entering the stream reaches the goal in the same life, and generally there are seven lives that stretch in front of him, through which he must pass ere the last step be taken. But it may be as well to remember perhaps, in reading all these books, that these phrases must not be taken too definitely; for the lives are effects, and these lives are not measured always by mortal births and mortal deaths; they are stages of progress perhaps, more often than human lives, but still they are sometimes measured between cradle and grave, although not necessarily. And these are said to be passed, life after life, without break; passing from one to another, passing onwards constantly without break in self-consciousness. And then beyond that first is another Portal, another Initiation; and as these lives are lived, certain last weaknesses of human nature are cast off one by one, cast off for ever, cast off completely; no longer now the incomplete labours of the Outer Court, no longer now the unfinished efforts, the unaccomplished endeavours. Here each work that is undertaken is perfectly achieved, each task that is begun is perfectly finished, and we see that in each of these stages certain definite fetters, as they are called, are cast aside, certain definite weaknesses for ever gotten rid of, as the disciple advances onwards to perfection, onwards to the full manifestation of the Divine in man.

Of the second Initiation it is said that he who passes it shall receive birth but once more. Only once more must he necessarily return, ere his compulsory rounds of births and deaths are over.

Many times he may return to voluntary reincarnation, but that will be of his own free will in service, and not by the binding to the wheel of births and deaths.   And as he passes through that stage and reaches the third Portal, the third great Initiation, he becomes the one who receives birth no more ; for in that very birth he shall pass through the fourth stage which takes him to the threshold of Nirvâna, and there can be no law that binds the Soul, for every fetter is broken and the Soul is free ; the fourth stage is that of the Arhat, where the last remaining fetters are utterly thrown aside.

Can we trace in any fashion at all these last stages, these four steps of Initiation ?   Can we realise, however dimly, what the work is which makes the passing of these four Gateways possible, and which makes the changed life on the other side ?   We have seen that the candidate is by no means perfect.   We see, in these published books that are lit by gleams from within the Temple, that still there are ten fetters of human weakness that one by one are to be cast off.   I do not now take them in detail, explaining each, for that would carry us too much within the Temple itself, and my work here is only in the Outer Court ; but, as you know, they may be stated, and I believe are likely before very long to be traced for you here one by one by

a competent hand. Let us then, without going into
detail, take them simply as guides for the moment,
and ask ourselves how it is that the demands are so
rigid before the threshold is crossed; why it is that
so much has to be done before this entrance into
the Temple is permitted, before Those who hold
the key of the Gate will throw it open when the
aspirant stands thereat for admission? It is easy,
I think, to see that the conditions we have already
studied must be partly fulfilled ere the aspirant can
cross the threshold. Every step that he takes on
the other side is a step that places greater and
greater powers within his grasp. On the other side
within the Temple his eyes will be open; on the
other side within the Temple he will be able to do
and live in a way that on the hither side is
impossible. The seeing, and the hearing, and the
doing, will make him a man very different from
the men around him, holding powers that they do
not share, having vision that is not theirs, knowledge
in which they have no part; he is to move amongst
them, but yet be partly not of them, different from
them while yet sharing in their common life. But
if that be so, it is needful to demand from him
that he shall truly be somewhat different from them
ere these powers shall be placed within his grasp;
for once possessed, he holds them and can use them.

Suppose, then, that he had the weaknesses so common in the outer world, suppose that he was easily irritated by the faults of those around him, suppose that he was easily thrown off his balance by the common events of daily life, suppose that his temper was not well under control, that his compassion was not growing, that his sympathy was not wide and deep, that when another injured him he felt anger instead of compassion, and irritation instead of forgiveness, suppose that he had little toleration and small patience, what would be the result of admitting such a man beyond the threshold, and allowing these powers which are superhuman, if you take the ordinary man as type, to pass at all, however imperfectly, within his grasp? Would there not be the danger, nay, the certainty, that these small faults so common in men and women in the world would bring about results of the nature of catastrophes; that if he were angry these fresh powers of the Soul he has gained—the strength of his will, the power of his thought— would make him a source of danger to his fellow-men as these forces were flung out and affected others? Supposing he were not tolerant, supposing he had not learnt to sympathise and to feel, to know the weaknesses he had conquered, and to understand the easiness of failure: what, then,

would be his position among men when he was able
to see their thoughts, when he was able to understand
and read their failings, and when those characters
which we veil from each other beneath the outer
appearance were no longer veiled to him, but stood
out clearly and definitely expressed (in that very
aura that I spoke of, which surrounds each
personality), so that he ever saw what people
were instead of what they appeared to be
in the outer world? Surely it would not
be right, nor just, nor well that such a power—
and it is one of the lowest on the Path—should be
placed in the hands of any one who has not learnt
by his own struggles to sympathise with the
weakest, and by the remembrance of his own faults
to give help and compassion, instead of condemna-
tion, to the weakest of his brethren whom he may
meet with in his daily life. Right is it and just
then that the demand should be rigid ere the
aspirant be permitted to step across the threshold;
fair and right is it that the demand should be made
upon him, and that he should be able to comply
with it; that there should be comparatively little
left, at least of these ordinary faults of men, ere
he steps within that mighty Temple where there is
room only for the helpers and the servants and the
lovers of mankind. And the task that he has to do

M

is also so gigantic a task, that it seems necessary that he shall have made fair progress ere he puts his hand to it at all : to get rid of every trace of human weakness, to gain all knowledge that can be gained within the limits of our system, to develop the powers which place all that knowledge within reach at will, so that by merely turning the attention anywhere everything that there can be known passes within the knowledge of the observer. For that and nothing less than that, remember, is the position of the Adept. The Adept is the " one who has no more to learn "; and Adeptship is but the last step on this Path that we are considering, which lies within the Temple, and which has to be trodden in so brief a space of time—a task so gigantic, an achievement so sublime, that were it not that men have done it, and are doing it, it would seem beyond possibility at all. For what would be this short span of lives from the ordinary standpoint for the making of such progress from the comparatively low stage which marks the first Initiation to that sublime height where the perfected Adepts are standing, the very flower and perfection of the evolution of Humanity? And since nothing less than that is the task which lies within the Temple, since nothing less than that achievement has to be accomplished, since not the slightest trace of human

weakness nor of human ignorance must cling to the
Arhat who is ready for the final Initiation, no
wonder that before the threshold is crossed there is
much for men to do, no wonder that the foundation
that we have spoken of, which is to support the
weight of so mighty a building and on which so
vast a superstructure is to be reared, must be made
strong and firm.   And remember, when the eyes
are opened the greatness of the task seems more
than in the days when the eyes were closed; that
to him who has begun to tread the Path, the Path
must seem far higher and longer than it can look to
those whose eyes are dim on the hither side of the
Gate; for he must see more clearly Those who are
beyond, and measure more accurately the distance
that separates him from Them.   And in the light of
that perfect glory, how dull must seem his own
achievement; how poor and weak everything he
can do, in the light of Their perfect strength; how
almost measureless his ignorance in the light of
Their perfect knowledge; and only four steps upon
the Path, only such brief tale of lives in which that
Path must be accomplished!   But the conditions
will be so different; and there must lie, one would
think, the possibility of the achievement; there
lies the strength perhaps of the feeling that the
men who have done it, and are doing it, passed in

crossing the threshold into a state of life so different from that they left behind, that that which would seem impossible here becomes to them possible there, and that which seemed so difficult becomes comparatively easy. For although we may not wholly realise all the conditions on the other side, there are some that it seems possible to think of, that show how different the life is within the Temple from that which lies without. For first of all in this change of conditions, there is the fact that the men who are there understand—and much lies in that word "understand." You remember those words that I just stopped short of intentionally, last week, in quoting the cry of triumph which came from the lips of the BUDDHA, when He proclaimed the end of bondage and the finding of liberty; how that cry to those who are in the outer world, telling them the cause of sorrow, spoke also of the ceasing of sorrow, and that that lay in the understanding of the reality.

> Ho! ye who suffer! know
> Ye suffer from yourselves. None else compels,
> None other holds you that ye live and die.

And the man who has crossed the threshold knows that to be very truth. Men suffer from themselves; they are not bound; and in under-

standing that, the whole world must change to his
vision, and all the difficulties of the Path will also
change their aspect. For once that we understand,
once that we realise, that all these troubles and
difficulties in the world grow from the world's
ignorance, that men suffer because they do not
know that they pass from life to life, and that they
grow so little because they do not know; that they
make so little of life because they do not know;
that they gain so little in each life because they do
not know; that all this wheel of births and deaths
on which they are bound holds them bound to it by
their want of knowledge, by their not realising that
they are really free if only they could understand—
when once the understanding comes, however
weakly, when once the understanding comes, not
indeed with the vision of the Enlightened One,
but still with full conviction, then the whole world
changes its aspect to this man who has crossed the
threshold, and looking back over the world with all
its sorrows and its miseries, with all its streaming
eyes and breaking hearts, he knows that there is
an end to sorrow, and that with the ceasing of
ignorance shall come the end of pain. And thus the
heartbreak of it is removed; though still the sorrow
may not be utterly outgrown, that which made it
despair and hopelessness has passed away from his

Soul for evermore. And that is not the only change of condition—that which gives not hope but certainty, not hope of the dawn but the rising sun, and the certainty of the coming day; that is not the only change of condition which lies on the other side of the threshold. One of the vast gains that he will have obtained in crossing over that threshold will be the gaining of a consciousness which shall not again be broken, over which death shall not have power, over which birth can no longer draw the sponge of oblivion. His consciousness for the lives that lie in front is to be consciousness continuous and unbroken, self-consciousness gained not again to be lost, self-consciousness achieved not again to be clouded; lost in truth it never can wholly be, when once it has begun in man; but it does not translate itself into the lower consciousness in the lives that lie on the worldly side of the Temple. In the lives that lie on the further side, within the Temple, the self-consciousness is an unbroken knowledge, so that that Soul can look before and after and feel itself strong in the knowledge of the immortal Self. And see how that will change all life; for what are two of the great sorrows of life which come to men, and which men cannot escape? Two of the worst sorrows that all have felt, and that all still feel, are those of separation and of death—separation which is made by space, when hundreds or thousand of miles may separate friend from friend, separation which is made by the change of condition when the veil of death has fallen between the Soul in the body and the Soul on the other side. But separation and death exist not for him who has crossed the threshold, as they existed for him while he was still in the outer world. To some extent he may feel them, to some extent— being still with the fetter of ignorance at least partially upon him—he may feel some pang of separation whether by distance or by death ; but it cannot really cloud his life, it cannot really break his consciousness ; it is only while he is in the body that the separation exists for him, and he may be out of the body at will, and go where space and time can no longer hold him. So that right out of his life are struck for all future lives these two of the great sufferings upon earth. No friend can again be lost to him, no death can again take from his side those who are knit to him in the bond of life. For to him neither separation nor death has a real existence ; those are evils of the past, and in their most terrible forms they are finished with for evermore.

Nor is that all of this enormous change of conditions in the life of the disciple. Not only has he this unbroken consciousness which makes it impossible that any can be utterly divided from him, but he knows that it also means that in these lives in front of him he will not slip back and feel as he has felt in the lives behind ; not again shall he come into the world unconscious, to waste perhaps half a life by not knowing what he seeks ; not again shall he come into the world ignorant of all, for the time blinded by the matter that veils him, and knowing not the true purpose of his life ; he will return again indeed, but return with knowledge ; return again indeed, but return for progress ; and it will be his own fault now if the progress be slackened, if he press not onwards. He has gained the consciousness that makes the progress possible, and any standing still or slackening will be his own fault, and in no sense a necessity of his life.

And then again his conditions will be changed by the new companionship into which he enters, companionship where there are no clouds, where no doubts and no suspicions can arise, companionship above all the mists of earth, where they have no place and cannot again disturb the Soul. For in crossing into the Temple he has come within sight of the great Teachers, in crossing the threshold he has come within the vision of the Masters, and in the possibility of the touch of such lofty companion-

ship, all life to him for evermore is changed. He
will have touched the permanent, and the transitory
cannot again shake him as in the days when he
knew not the Eternal. His feet are for evermore
upon the rock, and the waves will not be able to
wash him away from it, and give him again the
trouble of swimming in the tossing sea. So that
on this other side, mighty as is the task, the
conditions are so different that the task seems less
impossible, and we begin to understand why it
has been achieved in the past, and why it is being
achieved in the present; we begin to realise that
with such changes, such a Path, great as it is, may
still be trodden; and that these steps up the
mountain side, though they seem to raise the Soul
so high, and do raise it to heights so lofty, that
these steps may be taken with comparative swiftness
under conditions so different, and that the evolution
may well be rapid beyond almost all dreaming where
the powers of the Soul are thus unfolding and the
darkness has lifted, and the light is seen.

And these stages that are to be trodden under
these conditions, these steps that are yet to be
taken, and these fetters that are still to be cast
off—as we look at them we see that one after
another the last phases of human weakness are
disappearing, and the Soul shines out strong and

calm and pure. The delusion of the lower self is falling away, and all men are seen as one with the true Self. Doubt is vanishing, for it is replaced by knowledge; and as the Soul learns the reality of things, doubt becomes impossible for evermore. And all dependence on the outer that is transitory, that too will slip from off the Soul; for in this vivid contact with realities, all the outer things must take their due proportion, and it will learn how the outer matters but little, and how all the things which divide men are mere shadows, and not realities at all; that all differences of religions, and all efficacy of one ceremony more than another, nay, all exoteric rites and ceremonies, belong to the lower world, so that they are only illusive walls set up between the Souls of men; and these shadowy fetters will slip from the Soul that is learning, and these traces of human weakness will pass away. And the powers of the Soul will be unfolding, vision and hearing, the gaining of knowledge as yet undreamed of, flowing in from every side, and the whole Soul receptive; no longer limited by the senses as here below, no longer nearly all the Universe shut off, and only a small fragment of it here and there finding its way as knowledge to the Soul; but knowledge flowing in from every side and the whole surface of the Soul receptive to take it in; so that the gaining of the knowledge seems as it were a process of continually increasing life, and it comes constantly flowing into the Soul which has opened out to receive it from every side. And then still further on we faintly see that the Soul is getting rid of those etherealised shadows of desire that still seem to cling to it, the last touches as it were of the earthly life which might have power to retain. But as we reach the last of the Initiations, that stands before the highest, that which makes the man an Arhat, we find that it is all but impossible to understand at all, impossible to realise, what fetters there can be, what blemishes in a state so exalted; and truly it is written that the path of the Arhat "is difficult to understand, like that of birds in the air"; for like them he seems to leave no footprints, he seems to wing his way untouched, unfettered, in that high atmosphere wherein he moves; and from that region there comes down a sense of peace unshaken that nothing may disturb. For we are told that nothing can move him, nothing can shake him, that he stands there unassailable by any storm of earth, in a peace which nothing may avail to ruffle, in a serenity which nothing may avail to mar. Those who know the state have written of it, and in words which needs must be weak since they are human words, have said something of the characteristics of one like that in syllables that seem faintly to image out that lofty condition ; for they say that he is : —

Tolerant like the earth, like Indra's bolt ; he is like a lake without mud ; no new births are in store for him. His thought is quiet, quiet are his word and deed, when he has obtained freedom by true knowledge, when he has thus become a quiet man.

And it seems as though from that quiet there came down to us a sense of peace, of serenity, of unruffled calm, of that which naught may change or mar ; and we understand why of such one it should be written, that :

There is no suffering for him who has finished his journey, and abandoned grief, who has freed himself on all sides, and thrown off all fetters.

Such is the Arhat who stands at the summit of the Path ; such the one who has but one step more to take, and then shall have nothing more to learn ; such the goal and the Path which all may tread ; such the ending of the struggle, and the ending is perfect peace.*

In tracing the steps of the preliminary Path, in speaking in words all imperfect of what lies on

* The quotations are from the *Dhammapada*, chap. vii., " The Arhat."

the other side the Golden Gate, have I seemed
sometimes to speak too hardly, have I seemed to
paint the Path with colours too dark, too gloomy?
If it be so, then the fault is mine, and not the
fault of the Path; if it be so, then the error is in
the speaker, and not in that which feebly she has
striven to describe. For though there be difficulty
and struggle and suffering, it is true for all those
who enter the Outer Court, to say nothing of those
who have passed beyond the Golden Gate, that
when once they have entered within that Court,
they would not for aught that earth can give them
tread backwards to where they were before; and
for those who have passed across the threshold, is
there aught that earth could give of joy or promise,
that would make them even glance backwards at
the world they have left behind? For this Path
which stretches onward before us is a Path of
which the pains are better than earth's joys, and
the sufferings more glorious than earth's fruitions.
If you could press within the span of a human life
every joy that the lower earth could give; if you
could crowd it with pleasure, and with the giving
of the pleasure could also give the power to enjoy
without ceasing; if into that span of human life
you could bring all that men know of the joys of
the senses, nay, even what they know of the joys

of the intellect; if you could make it with no touch
of pain nor of weariness; if you could make it an
ideal life so far as earth can make ideal; then
beside the steps on the Path—no matter what those
steps may seem from the outer world—that life
of earth's joys would be sordid and dull in its
colouring, and its harmonies would be discords
beside the harmonies that lie beyond. For on this
Path each step that is taken is a step that is taken
for ever; each pain that is suffered on it is a pain
which, if it is felt, is welcome because of the
lesson that it gives. And in treading this Path it
grows brighter as ignorance lessens, it grows more
peaceful as weakness vanishes, it grows serener as
the vibrations of earth have less power to jar and
to disturb. What it is in its ending,—Those only
can tell who have ended; what it is at its goal,—
Those only may know who stand there. But even
those who are treading its earlier stages know that
its sorrow is joy as compared with the joy of earth,
and the very smallest of its flowers is worth every
jewel that earth could give. One gleam of the
Light which shines always upon it and that grows
ever brighter as the disciple treads onwards, one
gleam of that makes all earth's sunshine but as
darkness; they who tread it know the peace that
passeth understanding, the joy that earthly sorrow

can never take away, the rest that is on the rock that no earthquake may shiver, the place within the Temple where for ever there is bliss.

CPSIA information can be obtained
at www.ICGtesting.com
Printed in the USA
BVHW032317090822
644147BV00005B/133